Robert Shufflebotham

Photoshop CC

in easy steps

KT-161-677

For Windows and Mac

In easy steps is an imprint of In Easy Steps Limited
16 Hamilton Terrace · Holly Walk · Leamington Spa
Warwickshire · United Kingdom · CV32 4LY
www.ineasysteps.com

Copyright © 2014 by In Easy Steps Limited. All rights reserved. No part
of this book may be reproduced or transmitted in any form or by any
means, electronic or mechanical, including photocopying, recording,
or by any information storage or retrieval system, without prior
written permission from the publisher.

Notice of Liability
Every effort has been made to ensure that this book contains accurate
and current information. However, In Easy Steps Limited and the
author shall not be liable for any loss or damage suffered by readers
as a result of any information contained herein.

Trademarks
Photoshop® is a registered trademark of Adobe Systems Incorporated.
All other trademarks are acknowledged as belonging to their
respective companies.

In Easy Steps Limited supports The Forest Stewardship Council (FSC),
the leading international forest certification organisation. All our titles
that are printed on Greenpeace approved FSC certified paper carry the
FSC logo.

MIX
Paper from
responsible sources
FSC® C020837

Printed and bound in the United Kingdom

ISBN 978-1-84078-630-9

Contents

5 The Painting Tools 67

6 The Editing Tools 85

7 Selections 97

1 Basic Theory

Understanding the basics of color is important, if you are to get the best out of Photoshop.

Bitmaps and Vectors

Photoshop is an image-editing application, with a wealth of tools and commands for working on digital images or bitmaps. There are utilities for retouching, color correcting, compositing, and more. There are also over 100 functional and creative filters, which can be applied to entire images, selected areas, or specific layers.

A bitmap image consists of a rectangular grid, or raster, of pixels – very much like a mosaic in concept. When you edit a bitmap, you are editing the color values of individual pixels, or groups of pixels.

Image-editing applications differ fundamentally from vector-based applications, such as Adobe Illustrator. In these applications, you work with objects that can be moved, scaled, transformed, stacked, and deleted, as individual or grouped objects, but each exists as a complete, separate object all the time.

These applications are called vector drawing packages, as each object is defined by a mathematical formula. Because of this, they are resolution-independent – you can scale vector drawings up or down (either in the originating application or in a page layout application, such as QuarkXPress or Adobe InDesign) and they will still print smoothly and crisply.

You should always try to scan an image at, or slightly larger than, the size at which you intend to use it. This means you will avoid having to increase the size of the image, reducing its resolution and possibly its quality.

Scaled to 400%

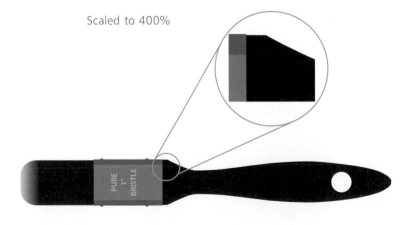

Vector drawing at actual size

In contrast, bitmaps are created at a set resolution – a fixed number of pixels per inch. If you scan an image at a specific resolution, then double its size, you are effectively halving its resolution (unless you add more pixels). You are likely to end up with a blocky, jagged image, as you have increased the size of the individual pixels that make up the bitmap image.

For digital images, more rather than less color information is usually desirable, as this means the image can represent more shades of color. Finer transitions between colors, and greater density of color, leads to a more realistic image.

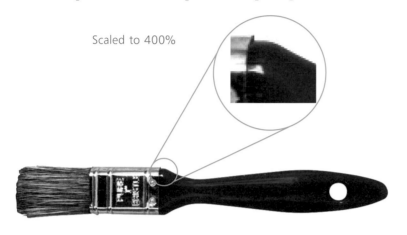

Scaled to 400%

300 ppi bitmap at actual size

Bitmaps and bit-depth

An important factor when the digital data of an image is captured, typically using a digital camera or by scanning, is its bit-depth. Bit-depth refers to the amount of digital storage space used to record information about the color of a pixel. The more bits you use, the more color information you can store to describe the color of a pixel – but the larger the file size you end up with.

To output realistic images using PostScript technology, an image should be able to represent 256 gray levels. A 24-bit scan is sufficient for recording 256 gray levels for each of the Red, Green and Blue channels (8-bits for each channel), resulting in a possible combination of over 16 million colors.

Ideally, when you work on images in Photoshop, you will do so using a monitor capable of displaying over 16 million colors. This ensures that you can see all the color detail in the image. Although you can work on images using only thousands of colors, for best results, especially where color reproduction is important, you need to work with as many colors as possible.

Photoshop can handle images that use 16-or 32-bits per channel, which originate from high-end digital cameras, scanners and microscopes. 16/32-bit per channel images contain a far greater range of colors than 8-bit per channel images. The disadvantage of working with such images is that their file sizes are also dramatically larger. The bit depth per channel of an image appears in the file name tab, or the title bar of the image window if you are working with floating windows:

Pixels and Resolution

Pixels

A pixel is the smallest element in a bitmap image captured by a digital camera or scanner. Pixel is short for "picture element". Zoom in on an image in Photoshop, and you will start to see the individual pixels – the fundamental building blocks – that make up the image. When working in Photoshop, you are moving, copying and editing pixels, changing their color, shade, and brightness to achieve a hugely varied set of changes to the image.

Resolution

A key factor, when working on bitmap images, is resolution. This is measured in pixels per inch (ppi).

Pixels can vary in size. If you have an image with a resolution of 100 ppi, each pixel would be 1/100th of an inch square. In an image with a resolution of 300 ppi, each pixel would be 1/300th of an inch square – giving a much finer, less blocky, result.

When working on images that will eventually be printed on a printing press, you need to work on high-resolution images. These are images whose resolution is twice the halftone screen frequency (measured in lines per inch – lpi) that will be used for final output – that is when you output to film or directly to plate.

For example, for a final output screen frequency of 150 lpi – a typical screen frequency used for glossy magazines – you need to capture or prepare your image at a resolution of 300 ppi.

Resolutions of double the screen frequency are important for images with fine lines, repeating patterns, or textures. You can achieve acceptable results, especially when printing at screen frequencies greater than 133 lpi, by using resolutions of 1½ times the final screen frequency.

To work with images for positional purposes only, as long as you can get accurate enough on-screen results and laser proofs, you can work with much lower resolutions.

Hot tip

Images intended for multimedia presentations, or the World Wide Web, need only be 72 ppi, which is effectively the screen resolution.

RGB and CMYK Color Models

You need to be aware of two color models, as you start working with Adobe Photoshop. These are the RGB (Red, Green, Blue) and CMYK (Cyan, Magenta, Yellow and blacK) color models.

RGB is important, because it mirrors the way the human eye perceives color. It is the model used by scanners and digital cameras to capture color information in digital format, and it is the way that your computer monitor describes color.

Hot tip

Strictly speaking, the 'K' in 'CMYK' stands for 'key'. In four-color printing the Cyan, Magenta and Yellow plates need to be carefully and accurately aligned – or 'keyed' – to the Black plate.

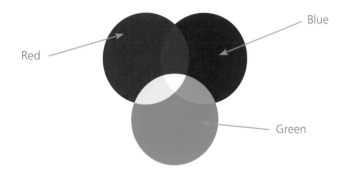

Red

Blue

Green

Red, green and blue are referred to as the "additive primaries". You can add varying proportions of the three colors, to produce millions of different colors – but still a more limited range (or "gamut") than in nature, due to the limitations of the monitor. If you add 100% of red, green and blue light together, you get white. You produce the "secondary" colors when you add red and blue to get magenta; green and blue to get cyan; red and green to get yellow.

The CMYK color model is referred to as the "subtractive" color model. It is important because this is the color model used by printing presses. If you subtract all cyan, magenta and yellow when printing, you end up with a complete absence of color – white.

Hot tip

On the printing press, cyan, magenta, yellow and black combine to simulate a huge variety of colors. Printers add black because, although in theory, if you combine 100% each of cyan, magenta and yellow, you produce black, in reality (because of impurities in the dyes) you only get a muddy brown.

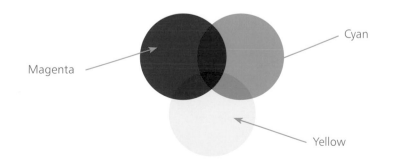

Magenta

Cyan

Yellow

11

Beware

When you convert from RGB to CMYK mode, Photoshop converts out-of-gamut colors (in this case, colors that can be seen on screen, but not printed) into their nearest printable equivalent.

Hot tip

The CIE (Commission Internationale de l'Eclairage) XYZ color model is a model that defines the visible spectrum that can be seen by a "standard" observer.

Colors with the same lightness value fall within an approximately triangular flat plane (the Visible Spectrum area in the diagram opposite). The x axis represents the amount of red in colors, and the y axis indicates the amount of green. The z axis represents the lightness of colors.

...cont'd

Color gamuts

Color gamut refers to the range of colors a specific device is capable of producing. There are millions of colors the eye can discern in the visible spectrum. Scanners, monitors, and printing presses cannot reproduce every color in the visible spectrum – the range of colors they are capable of producing is their gamut.

From the desktop publishing point of view, the process of capturing digital color information, viewing and manipulating this on-screen, and then finally printing the image using colored inks, is complicated, because the gamut of a color monitor is different to the gamut of CMYK and PANTONE inks. There are colors (especially vibrant yellows and deep blues) that can be displayed on a monitor, but cannot be printed using traditional CMYK inks.

Typically, you will work in RGB mode if the image is intended for use on the World Wide Web or in a multimedia presentation. You can work in CMYK or RGB mode if the image is intended for print, but you must remember to convert to CMYK mode before saving/exporting in EPS or TIFF file format, in order to use the image in a page layout application. Adobe InDesign can import CMYK or RGB images in native Photoshop (.PSD) file format.

CIE XYZ color model

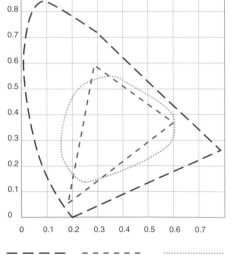

Visible Spectrum   Monitor   SWOP-CMYK

Color Management

No two devices that represent color, from digital camera to scanner, monitor to printer, will reproduce color in exactly the same way. The aim of a color management system is to ensure, as far as possible, that the colors you see on your screen are as close as possible to the colors you see in the finished work, whether in print or on screen.

Color management settings are available so that you can choose a color management workflow most suitable for your needs.

Using the Color Settings dialog box, you can define how you manage color in your images as you work in Photoshop.

1 To specify color management settings for your Photoshop working environment, launch Photoshop, then choose Edit > Color Settings (Ctrl/Command + Shift + K).

2 Choose the most appropriate setting for your intended final output, from the Settings pop-up list. For example, if you are using Photoshop for images that will be used in multimedia presentations, or on the World Wide Web, choose Web/Internet or Monitor Color options. If you are working with images that will be color separated then printed using CMYK inks, choose Europe or US Prepress defaults, as appropriate.

North America General Purpose 2	▾
Custom	
North America General Purpose 2	
Europe General Purpose 2	
Europe General Purpose 3	
Europe Prepress 2	
Europe Prepress 3	
Europe Web/Internet	
Europe Web/Internet 2	
Monitor Color	
North America General Purpose 2	
North America Prepress 2	
North America Web/Internet	

3 Only make changes to the default settings when you have gained experience in using Photoshop, and when you have a valid reason for making changes, or if you have consulted with your commercial printer and they have suggested changes to suit your specific output requirements.

Hot tip

If you use Photoshop with other applications in Creative Suite, such as InDesign and Illustrator, it is recommended that you synchronize color settings across the suite, using Adobe Bridge. In Bridge, choose Edit > Creative Suite Color Settings. Select a Color Settings option, then click Apply. (See pages 36-38 for information on Adobe Bridge.)

...cont'd

If you feel that you are not achieving good color in printed output, consult your commercial printer about creating custom settings for color management.

A CMS (Color Management System) is used to translate colors accurately, from one color device to another. It attempts to represent a color consistently, from the color space in which the image was created to the color space used at output, making adjustments so that color displays as consistently as possible across a range of monitors and other devices.

Recalibrate your monitor on a regular basis, as monitor performance can change over time.

4 To get a better understanding of how the settings work in the Color Settings dialog box, roll your cursor over the pop-up lists. The Description area at the bottom of the dialog box updates, with information on how the option affects the image.

5 Click the More Options button to access advanced color management settings. Only change advanced settings if you have a detailed understanding of color management.

Monitor Calibration

To make accurate and consistent judgements about the colors you see on your screen, you must calibrate your monitor. Monitor calibration creates a monitor profile that can be used as part of a color-managed workflow.

Hardware-based color calibration utilities are more accurate than the Adobe Gamma utility, previously available in Photoshop. There is a wide range of third-party monitor calibration suppliers – try doing an online search for "monitor calibration", or look for products such as "i1Basic Pro 2" from X-Rite, "Spyder4™ EXPRESS" from Datacolor, or "huey™PRO" from Pantone.

2 The Working Environment

This chapter covers the basics of the Photoshop working environment, getting you used to the Photoshop window, the Tool panel, other panels, and u number of standard Photoshop conventions and techniques that you will find useful, as you develop your Photoshop skills.

The Working Environment

There are three "screen modes" to choose from when working on images in Photoshop. The screen mode options are located at the bottom of the Photoshop Tool panel.

Full Screen Mode with Menu Bar is useful for working on individual images because it clears away the clutter of the Finder environment (Mac), or the Windows desktop. Use Full Screen Mode to see the image on a black background, without the distraction of other screen elements, and without any other colors interfering with the colors in your image.

In Full Screen Mode, press the Tab key to show/hide the Menu bar and panels.

You can use the keyboard shortcut – "F" – to cycle between screen modes.

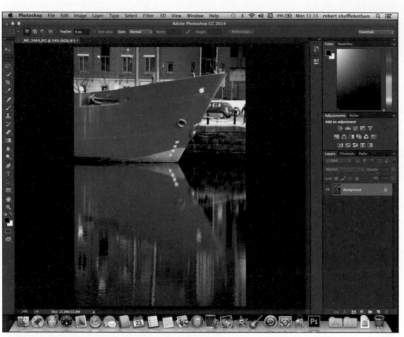

Standard Screen Mode

Full Screen Mode with Menu Bar

Full Screen Mode

Windows environment

The Windows environment offers identical functionality to the Macintosh environment, as you can see from a comparison of the Windows and Macintosh application window screen shots.

Command (often referred to as "Apple" on the Mac) and Ctrl (Windows), and Alt/option (Mac) and Alt (Windows) are used identically, as modifier keys. Shift is standard on both platforms.
This book uses Alt, with an uppercase "A", to denote both the Macintosh and Windows key of that name.

A floating image window

Title bar

Close button

Image

Scroll bars

View %

Resize box

Windows users can use the right mouse button to access context-sensitive menus; Mac users can hold down the Ctrl key and press their single mouse button.

See page 26 for information on working with "floating" windows.

17

Using the Tool Panel

There are a number of useful, general techniques that relate to choosing tools in the Tool panel, including those from the expanded range of hidden tool pop-ups.

Beware

You can only use the Rotate View tool if you have an OpenGL capable video card that provides graphics hardware acceleration. The tool allows you to rotate the on-screen representation of an image. This, however, is a temporary change to the angle at which you view the image when you are working on it – it is not the same as applying rotation to the actual pixels in the image (see page 50 for information on applying rotation to an image).

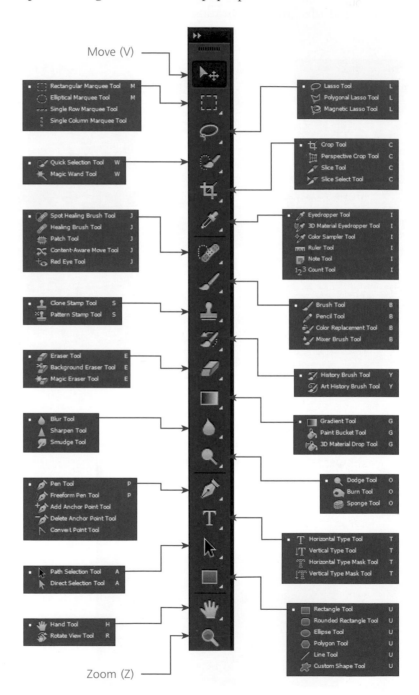

Move (V)

▣ Rectangular Marquee Tool	M
◯ Elliptical Marquee Tool	M
▭ Single Row Marquee Tool	
▯ Single Column Marquee Tool	

◯ Lasso Tool	L
◿ Polygonal Lasso Tool	L
◿ Magnetic Lasso Tool	L

✄ Quick Selection Tool	W
✦ Magic Wand Tool	W

◻ Crop Tool	C
◻ Perspective Crop Tool	C
✄ Slice Tool	C
✄ Slice Select Tool	C

✎ Spot Healing Brush Tool	J
✎ Healing Brush Tool	J
▦ Patch Tool	J
✄ Content-Aware Move Tool	J
✛ Red Eye Tool	J

✎ Eyedropper Tool	I
✎ 3D Material Eyedropper Tool	I
✦ Color Sampler Tool	I
▥ Ruler Tool	I
▦ Note Tool	I
1₂3 Count Tool	I

▣ Clone Stamp Tool	S
▣ Pattern Stamp Tool	S

✎ Brush Tool	B
✎ Pencil Tool	B
✎ Color Replacement Tool	B
✎ Mixer Brush Tool	B

✎ Eraser Tool	E
✎ Background Eraser Tool	E
✦ Magic Eraser Tool	E

✎ History Brush Tool	Y
✎ Art History Brush Tool	Y

◗ Blur Tool	
▲ Sharpen Tool	
◗ Smudge Tool	

▣ Gradient Tool	G
◗ Paint Bucket Tool	G
◗ 3D Material Drop Tool	G

✎ Pen Tool	P
✎ Freeform Pen Tool	P
✛ Add Anchor Point Tool	
✎ Delete Anchor Point Tool	
▷ Convert Point Tool	

◯ Dodge Tool	O
◗ Burn Tool	O
◯ Sponge Tool	O

T Horizontal Type Tool	T
↕T Vertical Type Tool	T
T Horizontal Type Mask Tool	T
T Vertical Type Mask Tool	T

▷ Path Selection Tool	A
▷ Direct Selection Tool	A

▭ Rectangle Tool	U
▭ Rounded Rectangle Tool	U
◯ Ellipse Tool	U
⬠ Polygon Tool	U
╱ Line Tool	U
✦ Custom Shape Tool	U

✋ Hand Tool	H
✋ Rotate View Tool	R

Zoom (Z)

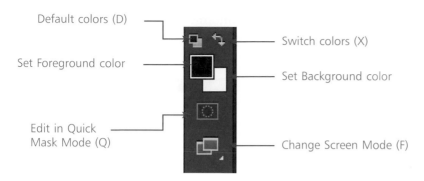

Default colors (D)

Switch colors (X)

Set Foreground color

Set Background color

Edit in Quick
Mask Mode (Q)

Change Screen Mode (F)

Tool panel techniques

1 Press the keyboard shortcut listed in a tool pop-up, to select tools.

2 Click and hold on any tool with a small triangle in the bottom right corner, to see all tools in that tool group.

3 Hold down Alt/option and click on any tool in a tool group, to cycle through the available tools. Alternatively, hold down Shift, then press the keyboard shortcut for that tool group a number of times. For example, press "O" three times to cycle through all the tools in the Dodge tool group.

4 Press Tab to hide/show all panels, including the Tool panel. Hold down Shift, then press the Tab key to hide/show all panels except the Tool panel.

5 Press Caps Lock to change the painting or brush size cursor to a precise crosshair cursor, which indicates the center of the painting tool. Press Caps Lock again to return to the standard cursor display.

6 When you select a tool in the Tool panel, the Options bar, extending across the top of the Photoshop window, updates according to the tool you select. Get into the habit of checking the settings in the Options bar before you use the tool.

Hot tip

Choose Edit > Preferences > Cursors (Windows), or Photoshop > Preferences > Cursors (Mac), to change the default appearance of painting and other cursors.

Document and Scratch Sizes

The Sizes bar is useful for monitoring disk space and memory considerations, as you work on your images.

Document Sizes

With Document Sizes selected, you see two numbers separated by a slash. The first number is the size of the image with all layers flattened. The second number may be larger, and represents the file storage size whilst the image contains additional layers and/or alpha channels you may have set up. In images that consist of only a single layer, with no additional channels, both numbers are the same.

Scratch Sizes

The Scratch disk is an underlying technical detail that you should be aware of when using Photoshop. The Scratch disk is a designated hard disk that Photoshop uses as "virtual" memory, if it runs out of memory (RAM) whilst working on one or more images.

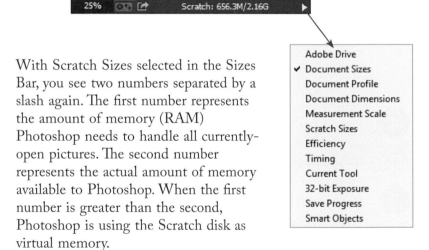

With Scratch Sizes selected in the Sizes Bar, you see two numbers separated by a slash again. The first number represents the amount of memory (RAM) Photoshop needs to handle all currently-open pictures. The second number represents the actual amount of memory available to Photoshop. When the first number is greater than the second, Photoshop is using the Scratch disk as virtual memory.

As a general rule of thumb, when working in Photoshop, you should have free disk space of at least 3-5 times the file size of the image you are working on. This is because Photoshop makes use of the Scratch disk as virtual memory, and because Photoshop needs to hold more than one copy of the image you are working on, for the Undo, Revert, and History panel functions.

Hot tip

Choose Edit (Windows) or Photoshop (Mac), then select Preferences > Performance, if you want to change the default amount of RAM allocated to Photoshop.

Hot tip

Choose Edit (Windows) or Photoshop (Mac), then select Preferences > Performance, to specify the hard disk(s) you want Photoshop to use as a Scratch disk. Ideally, the primary Scratch disk should be your fastest hard drive.

Hot tip

To improve performance when working with large image files, a Scratch disk should be on a different drive to the one where the image is located.

Ruler Guides and Grids

You can show a grid in your image window, to help with alignment and measuring, and you can also drag in ruler guides. Both

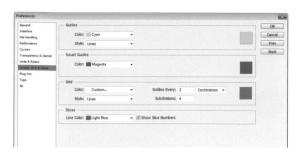

sets of guides are non-printing. Customize the appearance of the grid and guides by choosing Edit (Windows) or Photoshop (Mac), then selecting Preferences > Guides, Grid & Slices.

Hot tip

Make sure you select View > Snap To > Guides/Grid, if you want cursors and selections to snap to guides and the grid. These options are very useful for aligning elements accurately.

1 To show or hide the grid, choose View > Show > Grid.

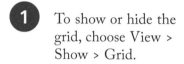

2 To create a ruler guide, first choose View > Rulers to display the rulers along the top and left edges of the image window.

Position your cursor in a ruler, and then click and drag onto your image to create either a vertical or horizontal guide.

Hot tip

Use keyboard shortcuts: Ctrl/Command + ; to Hide/ Show ruler guides Ctrl/Command + ' to Hide/ Show the grid.

3 To reposition a ruler guide, select the Move tool, position your cursor on a guide, then click and drag. The cursor changes to a bi-directional arrow when

you pick up a guide. To remove a ruler guide, drag the ruler guide back into the ruler it came from. Alternatively, choose View > Clear Guides to remove all guides.

4 To temporarily hide any grid or guides, in order to preview the image without the clutter of non-printing guides, choose View > Extras (Ctrl/Command + H). Use the same command to bring back the guides and grid.

Beware

Take care, when repositioning ruler guides, that you don't accidentally reposition an entire layer. Make sure you see the bi-directional arrows, which indicates that you are dragging a guide.

Zooming and Moving Around

Use any combination of the Navigator panel, the Zoom tool, the Hand tool, and the scroll bars, for moving around and zooming in and out of your image.

Hot tip

With the Zoom tool selected, position the cursor where you want to zoom in, then press and hold down the mouse button to access a continuous zoom.

1 Choose Window > Navigator to show the Navigator panel, if it is not already visible. In the panel, you can double-click the % entry box, enter a zoom % (0.08-3200), then press Return/Enter. Alternatively, drag the zoom slider to the right to zoom in, or to the left to zoom out. Each time you change your zoom level, the view in the Preview area updates.

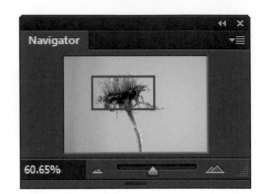

Hot tip

Hold down Ctrl/Command and the Spacebar to temporarily access the Zoom tool, with any other tool selected. Add the Alt/option key to the above combination to zoom out.

2 Drag the red View box in the Preview area to move to different areas of your image quickly.

3 To use the Zoom tool, select it, position your cursor on the image, and click to zoom in on the area around your cursor, in preset increments. With the Zoom tool selected, hold down Alt/option. The cursor changes to the zoom out cursor; click to zoom out in the preset increments.

4 With the Zoom tool selected, you can also click and drag to define the area you want to zoom in on.

5 You can use the Hand tool, in addition to using the scroll bars, to move around your image when you have zoomed in on it. Select the tool, position your cursor on the image, then click and drag to reposition.

Hot tip

With any other tool selected, hold down the Spacebar to temporarily access the Hand tool. Avoid using this technique if you are working with text.

The Info Panel

The Info panel (Window > Info) provides useful numerical read-outs, relative to the position of the cursor on your image.

You can use it as an on-screen densitometer, to examine color values at the cursor. There are two color read-outs. As a default, the first color read-out is the actual color under the cursor. For example, a read-out of red, green, and blue color components in an RGB image. The default second read-out is for cyan, magenta, yellow, and black values.

The panel also displays x and y coordinates, giving the precise location of the cursor as it moves over the image.

If you create a selection, there is a read out of the width and height of the selection. The panel also displays values for some options, such as rotating, skewing and scaling selections.

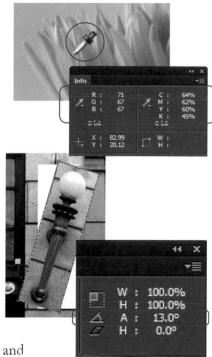

Beware

An exclamation mark next to the CMYK readouts indicates that a color is outside the printable CMYK gamut, or range of colors:

23

1. To change the default settings for the Info Panel, choose Panel Options from the Info panel menu ( ).

2. Use the Mode pop-ups to choose the first and second color read-outs.

3. You can also choose a unit of measurement for mouse coordinates.

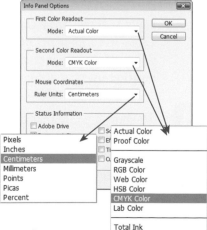

Panel Techniques

For the Essentials workspace, the main default Panel dock on the right of the Photoshop window contains seven panels, with a further two panel icons for the History and the Properties panel. You can expand or collapse the display of the Panel dock, and you can rearrange panels to suit your individual working preferences. In its default arrangement, the main dock is expanded.

Hot tip

Use the Workspace Switcher pop-up menu,

towards the top right of the Photoshop window, to choose an arrangement of panels that most closely suits your needs as you work. Then, if you move and hide panels as you work, you can restore the default arrangement for a particular workspace by selecting Reset ... from the pop-up menu.

24

Hot tip

For some panels, you can drag the Resize icon (▦), in the bottom right corner of a panel, to increase/decrease its size.

Hot tip

To manually resize the width of the Panel dock, position your cursor on the left edge of the dock. Drag when you see the bi-directional arrow cursor (⟺).

1 Click the Collapse to Icons button (▶▶) to shrink the display of panels to panel tabs. To expand the Panel dock, click the Expand Panels button (◀◀) in the top right corner of the dock.

2 Click on a panel tab to make the panel active, so that its controls become available.

3 To remove a panel from the dock, make sure the panel is active, then choose Close from its panel menu. Go to the Window menu, then select the panel name to restore it to its previous position on your screen.

4 To show a panel that does not appear in the default Panel dock, go to the Window menu, then select the panel name. The panel appears in a secondary dock, to the left of the main default dock. You can manage the appearance of panels in the secondary dock by using the same techniques you use for the main dock.

Panel Groups

The panels in the panel dock are initially arranged in tab groups. For example, Layers, Channels, and Paths form a tab group. There are a number of techniques you can use to control the appearance of tab groups.

1 To hide all panels in a tab group, select Close Tab Group, from the panel menu () of the active panel. If you hide a complete group, selecting any of the panels from the Window menu re-displays the full tab group.

2 To collapse the display to tabs only, double-click anywhere on the tab name. Click once on a collapsed panel tab to expand the panel group.

Floating and combining panels

To provide complete flexibility in the way you manage panels, each panel can be made into a floating panel, or you can combine panels into your own custom groupings.

1 To create a floating panel, position your cursor on the panel's tab, then drag the panel out from the group – typically into the image window. To reposition the floating panel, drag its tab, or the panel's gray title bar.

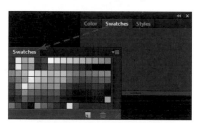

2 To combine a panel with another panel group, drag the panel's tab or gray title bar into the panel group. Release the mouse when the panel group highlights in blue.

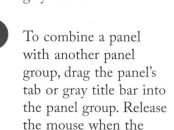

Hot tip

All panels have a panel menu, for accessing a range of commands or options relevant to the panel. Click the panel menu button (▾≡) to access the panel menu.

Hot tip

Press the Tab key to hide/show all panels, including the Tool panel. Hold down Shift, then press Tab to hide/show currently visible panels, with the exception of the Tool panel.

Hot tip

Choose Window > Workspace > New Workspace, to save the current position of your panels. Enter a name for this workspace arrangement in the Save Workspace dialog box. Choose Window > Workspace, then select the name of the workspace, to reset panels to this arrangement.

25

Controlling the Workspace

It is very common, when working in Photoshop, to have more than one image open at a time. Image or document windows are tabbed by default.

1 As you open images, each new document displays a file name tab below the Options bar. Click a tab to make the window active. Click the Close button (☒) to close a document.

2 To view images in separate floating windows, choose Window > Arrange > Float All in Windows. Click on any part of a document window to make it active, or go to the Window menu and select the image's file name from those listed at the bottom of the menu.

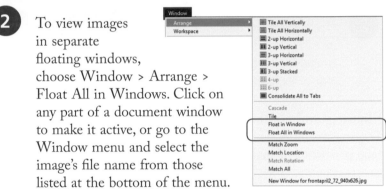

On the Mac, choose Window > Application Frame to create an application window that can be resized, in the same way that you can in Windows. When you select this option, the default Title bar, which runs along the top of the document tabs, disappears.

3 To change the default setting for the arrangement of document windows, from tabbed to floating, choose Edit > Preferences > Interface (Windows) or Photoshop > Preferences > Interface (Mac), then deselect the Open Documents as Tabs checkbox.

To move from floating document windows to tabbed, choose Window > Arrange > Consolidate All to Tabs.

4 Use the top and middle set of buttons in the Arrange Documents pop-up menu to tile document windows into an arrangement that suits you, so that you can evaluate and compare multiple images.

Save and Load Custom Settings

The Swatches, Styles and Actions panels, the Adjustment panels, the Brushes presets panel, along with dialog boxes such as Duotones, have Save and Load options that allow you to save custom settings made in the panel or dialog box, and then load them into Photoshop when required. The following example uses the Swatches panel.

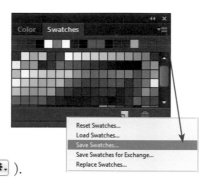

1 After creating a custom Swatches panel (see page 66), choose Save Swatches in the panel menu. In a dialog box, choose Save Preset, from the Presets pop-up menu ( ).

2 The Save dialog box prompts you for a a file name and location in which to save the settings. The default Color Swatches folder is in the Presets folder,

within the Photoshop CC folder. The extension for a Color Swatches file is .aco. Make sure you save the file with the correct extension.

3 To load previously-saved settings, choose Load Swatches from the panel menu. In a dialog box, select Load Presets from the Presets pop-up menu ( ). Then specify the location of the settings you previously saved. Click on the settings file name, then click Open. Load Swatches adds the new swatches to the existing swatches in the panel.

Hot tip

In the Brushes panel, select a brush set from the bottom of the Brushes panel menu. Try Assorted Brushes as a starting point for experimenting with different brush types.

Hot tip

Choose Reset Swatches in the panel menu to restore settings to their original defaults.

Beware

The exact appearance of the Page Setup dialog box varies according to the printer.

Hot tip

In the Print dialog box, click the Expand/Collapse triangle for Printing Marks to specify additional printed information, such as Crop Marks and Registration Marks. As you switch on the various options, they appear in the preview area.
Use the Expand/Collapse triangles in the scroll box to the right of the dialog box to reveal controls for Position and Size, Color Management, Printing Marks and so on.

Beware

In the Print dialog box, only change Color Management options if you are not satisfied with your printed output. Note the settings you change, so you can compare results and return to previous settings if necessary.

Printing

When you have made all the necessary edits and adjustments to an image, you are ready to print. The Print dialog box has a color managed thumbnail preview of the image, and you can access additional print features and a preview of the image as it will print on the specified paper size.

1 Choose File > Print. Make sure the correct printer is selected from the Printer pop-up menu. Enter the number of copies you want to print. Some options are available only if you are printing to a PostScript printer.

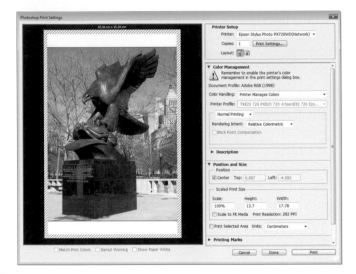

2 Click the Print Settings button to set controls specific to your printer. In particular, make sure the Paper Type and Size are set correctly, check that the orientation is appropriate, and select a quality option. Refer to the manufacturer's manual for information on the options available for the printer. Click OK.

3 If necessary, click the Scale to Fit Media checkbox, to reduce the size of the image so that it fits onto the specified paper size.

4 Click Print in the Print Settings dialog box to print a copy of the image. Click Done if you want to save changes in the dialog box and return to the image without printing it.

The History Panel

Every time you modify an image, Photoshop records this as a new state in the History panel. The panel records the last 20 states of the image. Use the History panel to return to a previous state of the image within the current work session. The most recent state of the image appears at the bottom of the list in the panel.

You can also use the keyboard shortcuts Ctrl/Command + Shift + Z to move to the next state. Use Ctrl/Command + Alt/option + Z to move to the previous state.

1 To return to a previous state of the image, click on a state in the History panel. The image reverts to that stage of the work session. States, after the state you click on, are dimmed. These subsequent states are discarded if you continue to work from the selected state.

2 Alternatively, choose Step Forward/Step Backward from the panel menu ( ), to move sequentially through the states.

Deleting states
Delete states from the History panel to remove the changes to the image recorded by that state, and all subsequent states.

1 To delete a history state, click on its name, then choose Delete from the panel menu. Alternatively, drag the state into the Trash can icon at the bottom of the panel.

Step Forward	Shift+Ctrl+Z
Step Backward	Alt+Ctrl+Z
New Snapshot...	
Delete	
Clear History	
New Document	
History Options...	
Close	
Close Tab Group	

Both techniques for deleting states delete the selected state, and all states that occur after it. In other words, you are reverting to the state of the image previous to the state you delete.

Clearing states
Clearing states leaves the image at its current state, but removes all previous states from the History panel.

1 To clear the History panel, use the panel menu to choose Clear History. All recorded states are deleted from the History panel, leaving the image at its most recent state.

Use File > Revert to revert to the state of your image as it was when you last did a File > Save. The Revert command appears as a state in the History panel.

You can use Edit > Undo to cancel the Clear History command, but not the Purge states commands.

Beware

Snapshots record the state of an image at a particular point in time. They are useful if you want to retain a particular state of the image, so that you can return to it at a later stage.

Beware

As soon as you close an image, all recorded history states and snapshots are discarded.

...cont'd

Purging states

Purging states is useful if you get a low memory message. This is typically because the Undo buffer is becoming full, with the changes to the image that it is having to record. When you purge states, they are deleted from the Undo buffer, freeing up memory.

1 To purge states, hold down Alt/option, then choose Clear History from the panel menu in the History panel. This command purges history states from the active image. Choose Edit > Purge > Histories if you want to purge all history states for all open images.

Snapshots

An initial "snapshot" is created by default, when you open an image. This appears at the top of the History panel. As you work on the image, the History panel records the results of the last 20 operations performed. Older states of the image are automatically deleted, to keep memory free for Photoshop. You can keep particular states of an image during a work session by making additional snapshots.

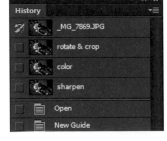

1 To create additional snapshots, click on any state in the History panel. Choose New Snapshot from the panel menu. In the New Snapshot dialog box, enter a name. Click OK in the dialog box. A new snapshot is added in the top section of the History panel.

2 Click on a snapshot to revert to the state of the image when the snapshot was created. If you then continue to work on the image, all history states are lost.

3 To delete a snapshot, click once on the snapshot to select it, then click on the Trash can icon at the bottom of the panel.

3 Open and Save Files

Opening and converting files to a wide range of formats to suit varied output requirements is one of Photoshop's great strengths. This chapter covers a range of essential techniques for opening and saving images in Photoshop.

Opening Images in Photoshop

After you launch Photoshop, you can open images using the File menu. Adobe Bridge provides a powerful and flexible alternative method for locating and opening images (see pages 36-38 for further information).

In the Windows desktop environment, right-click an image icon, choose Open With > Choose Default Program, then select Photoshop CC, so that when you subsequently double-click any file icon of the same type, Photoshop launches automatically.

1 To open an image from within Photoshop, choose File > Open. This takes you into the Open dialog box. Navigate through folders and sub-folders, as necessary, to locate the file you wish to open, click on the file name to select it, then click Open. Alternatively, just double-click the file name.

2 Select Show All Readable Documents (Mac), or choose All Formats from the Files of type pop-up (Windows), to show all files in the selected folder.

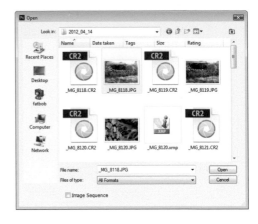

3 You can also open recently-opened files by choosing File > Open Recent. Select a file from the list.

4 (Mac) To search for a file that you want to open from within the Open dialog box, use the search bar in the top right of the Open dialog box.

Choose Edit > Preferences > File Handling (Windows), or Photoshop Preferences > File Handling (Mac), then enter a number for Recent File List Contains to control the number of files that appear in the Open Recent files sub-menu.

Scanning into Photoshop

You can scan into Photoshop using the File > Import sub-menu. Make sure you install the scanning software for your scanner before you begin.

1 To create a scan from within Photoshop, choose File > Import, then select the appropriate scanner from the sub-menu.

Typically, you can either scan using the scanner's default settings, or you can customize settings, including: scan mode (grayscale, color, line art, etc.), resolution, scale, contrast, brightness and gamma. Refer to your scanning software manual for details on the controls available.

Many of the scanning controls have equivalent functions in Photoshop. Scanning options vary from scanner to scanner, but you should be able to specify whether you are scanning a transparency or a photograph. The other essential decisions you need to make at this stage are image mode, resolution, and scale. You may also need to specify a crop area in the preview window.

2 Click the Scan button. Wait until the scanning process finishes and the image appears in an untitled Photoshop window. Save the image.

If you want to import an image using the TWAIN interface, first install the TWAIN plug-in, which can be downloaded from: http://download. adobe.com/pub/adobe/ photoshop/win/13.x/ Win_Optional_Plug- ins.zip (Win), or http:// download.adobe.com/ pub/adobe/photoshop/ mac/13.x/Optional_Plug_ Ins_Release.dmg (Mac) TWAIN is not available for Photoshop in 64-bit mode.

For WIA (Windows Image Acquisition) - compliant scanners, choose File > Import > WIA Support. In the WIA Support dialog box, click the Browse button to specify a location in which to save the scanned image, then click the Start button. Select your scanner in the Select Device dialog box. Click OK to begin the scan. Select scanner-specific options, as necessary. Refer to the manufacturer's manual for detailed information on the options available.

Opening and Placing EPS files

EPS stands for Encapsulated Postscript. EPS files can contain bitmap as well as vector information. EPS files, created in applications such as Adobe Illustrator, typically contain object-oriented, or "vector" format, information.

Opening an Illustrator EPS file

When you open an EPS file in Photoshop, it is rasterized, i.e. the vector information is converted into Photoshop's pixel-based format.

Hot tip

You can also use File > Open to open native Illustrator (.ai) files as a Photoshop document:

cashflow.ai

1 To open an EPS file as a new document, choose File > Open. Locate and highlight the EPS file you want to open, then click the Open button. Alternatively, double-click the file name.

2 In the Rasterize dialog box, enter new dimensions for Width and Height, if required. Enter the resolution required for your final output device, and choose an image mode from the Mode pop-up menu.

Hot tip

An embedded Photoshop file (.psd) with layers retains its original layer structure when you edit it by double-clicking the smart object layer.

3 Select the Constrain Proportions box, to keep the original proportions of the EPS. Select Anti-aliased to slightly blur pixels along edges, to avoid unwanted jagged edges. Click OK. The EPS appears in its own image window. It is now a bitmap image.

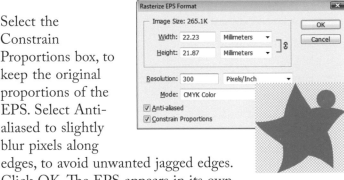

Placing an embedded Photoshop or Illustrator file

You can also "place" another Photoshop file or an Illustrator file into an open Photoshop document. The placed artwork appears on a new Smart Objects layer. (See page 132 for information on placing Photoshop and Illustrator artwork as external linked files.)

Hot tip

Before you accept the placed EPS, you can also use the Options bar to change position, size, rotation, and skew values numerically for the file.

1 First, create a new Photoshop document.

...cont'd

2 Choose File > Place Embedded. Use the Place dialog box to specify the location and name of the file you want to place, then click the Place button.

3 A bounding box, with eight "handles" and a cross through the placed image, appears in the Photoshop image window.

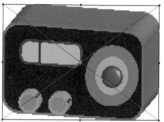

4 If necessary, drag a corner handle to resize the placed image. Hold down Shift as you drag, to maintain proportions. Position your cursor inside the bounding box of the placed image, and drag to reposition the image.

5 When you are satisfied, click the Commit button in the Options bar, press Return/Enter, or double-click inside the bounding box.

6 A "flattened" version of a Photoshop file with layers is placed on a new Smart Object layer. However, when you double click an embedded layered Photoshop file it retains its layer structure for editing as a smart object. Similarly, all objects in an embedded Illustrator file can be manipulated when you edit the smart object layer. (See page 130-131 for further information on working with Smart Object layers.)

To create anti-aliased edges for a placed EPS, you must select the Anti-aliased option in the Options bar before you click the Accept button.

If you don't want to accept the placed image, with the bounding box still visible, press the Esc key. If you have already placed the image, you can delete the new layer (see page 118).

You can copy vector artwork from Illustrator into Photoshop, using the clipboard. In Illustrator, copy selected artwork using Edit > Copy, then, in Photoshop, choose Edit > Paste. Choose Path in the Paste dialog box, to import the artwork as paths in the Paths panel:

35

Bridge

Adobe Bridge provides a powerful, visual environment for locating, organizing, and tracking image files and other digital assets on your system. Choose File > Browse in Bridge to launch Bridge from within Photoshop.

Hot tip

You can launch Bridge as a standalone application, as you would launch any other application – from the Start > Programs menu in Windows, or from the Applications folder on the Mac.

Favorites view

Favorites view gives you quick access to image folders you use frequently. You can create your own favorites folders. Setting up favorites can save you a lot of time when navigating to folders that you use on a regular basis.

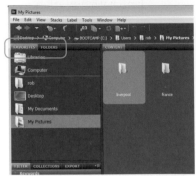

Hot tip

You can create a Favorites folder from the Folders tab. Navigate to a specific folder, position your cursor on the folder, then right-click (Windows) or Ctrl + click (Mac). Select Add to Favorites, from the context menu.

1 To create a new favorites folder, click the Favorites tab, then click the Computer icon. Navigate to the folder in the Contents pane. Click once on the folder to select it, then drag it into the Favorites pane.

2 To remove a folder from the Favorites pane, position your cursor on the folder, then right-click (Windows) or Ctrl + click (Mac). Select Remove from Favorites from the context menu.

Folders view

Click the Folders tab to view, manage, sort, and open images on your system. You can also use the Folder view to create new folders, and to rename, move, delete and rank image files.

Hot tip

To move a file, position your cursor on the image thumbnail in the Content pane, then drag it to a different folder in the Folder panel of the Bridge window. To copy a file to a new location, hold down Ctrl (Win) or Alt/option (Mac), then drag it to a different folder.

1 In the Bridge window, click the Folder tab. Use the Folder pane to navigate to specific folders on your hard disk, using standard Windows/Macintosh techniques.

2 The Content pane in the middle of the workspace displays thumbnail previews of the contents in the selected folder. When you click on a thumbnail in the Content pane, a larger version of the image appears in the Preview pane.

Drag the Thumbnail Size slider, at the bottom of the window, to control the size of thumbnail previews in the contents area.

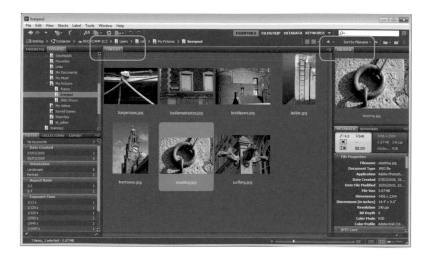

The three buttons in the bottom right of the Bridge window allow you to control the arrangement and readouts for thumbnails in the Content pane. You can view by thumbnail, details, and list:

3 Essentials is the default workspace. Use the Workspace pop-up menu, or click on one of the visible workspace options, to change the arrangement of panes in Bridge to suit the way you work.

4 File information for a selected thumbnail appears in the Metadata and Keywords panes. You can also use options from the panel menu for each tab, to add and edit metadata and keyword information for your image files. Use the Expand/Collapse triangles (▶) to display/ hide information for each category.

Choose an option from the View > Sort sub-menu, to control the way image thumbnails are ordered in the Preview pane.

37

...cont'd

Hot tip

To delete a file, click on the file thumbnail to select it, then either click the Trash can icon in the Toolbar, or drag the file onto the Trash can.

5 To open a file from the Content area, click on an image thumbnail to select it, then press the Enter/Return key. You can also double-click a thumbnail. If you open a Camera Raw image, it opens in the Camera Raw dialog box. (See pages 39-40 for information on Camera Raw.)

6 To create a 1-5 star ranking for a selected thumbnail, click a dot below the thumbnail to convert it to a star. To remove stars, click the star to the left of the star you want to remove, or click to the left of all the stars to remove the ranking. Alternatively, use the Label menu to apply star ratings to a selected image.

Hot tip

Choose Filmstrip workspace, (which provides a large preview area), then select two or more thumbnails in the Contents pane, to compare them in the Preview area.

7 Use the Filter pane to display only thumbnails with a specific rating. If necessary, click the Ratings expand triangle, then click to the left of the star ratings to display images with a particular rating.

8 To display thumbnails in the Content pane according to their rank, choose View > Sort > By Rating. Alternatively, use the Sort By pop-up menu at the top of the window.

Hot tip

Choose File > Get Photos from Camera, or click the Get Photos from Camera button ( ) to download images from a connected camera onto your computer and directly into Bridge.

9 You can apply color labels to selected thumbnails, by choosing a label from the Labels menu. You can then use the Filter pane to sort and filter thumbnails using label criteria.

Adobe Camera Raw

When you capture a raw image, the camera does not process the color data in the image, apply compression settings, such as JPEG, make tonal adjustments, nor set white balance and other values. Using the Camera Raw dialog box gives you precise control over how you manipulate the raw digital color information captured by the camera.

1 To open a camera raw image, launch Bridge. (See pages 36-38 for information on using Bridge.) Double-click a camera raw image in Bridge, to open the image in the Camera Raw window.

2 From Photoshop, choose File > Open. Browse to a Camera Raw file, select it, then click the Open button.

The Camera Raw window contains an extensive range of commands for manipulating the raw image data captured by the camera.

3 The Histogram, in the top right corner of the window, provides visual feedback on changes you make to settings in the tabbed control panels area of the window in real time. When you first start to work with Camera Raw images, begin by using the Basic tab ( ) controls to

Hot tip

You can recognize a camera raw file in Bridge by the .CR file extension:

In the Photoshop Open dialog box by the camera raw file icon:

Hot tip

If you double-click a Camera Raw file icon in the desktop environment, the image opens in the Camera Raw dialog box.

Hot tip

Click the Toggle Full Screen button to enlarge the Camera Raw window to fill the screen to make the most of your available screen space.

...cont'd

The tabbed controls
available in the Camera
Raw dialog box are:
- Basic
- Tone Curve
- Detail
- HSL/Grayscale
- Split Toning
- Lens Correction
- Effects
- Camera Calibration
- Presets
- Snapshots

A processed image icon
( ) appears in Bridge
thumbnails after you edit
settings for a Camera
Raw file.

DNG – Digital Negative file
format is a non-proprietary
format, developed by
Adobe, which should
ensure that images archived
in this format remain easily
accessible in the future.

adjust white balance, tone, and saturation. More advanced controls provided in the remaining tabs allow you to fine tune your initial settings (see Hot tip).

4 The Histogram info area provides useful information about the camera, and some of the exposure settings used to capture the image.

5 The Tool Bar, running along the top of the window, provides basic tools for zooming, panning, setting color sample points, cropping, straightening, and rotating, which are similar to controls available within Photoshop. There is also a Red Eye Removal tool, a Spot Removal tool, an Adjustment Brush, and a Graduated Filter control.

6 Use the Zoom controls at the bottom left of the window to zoom in or out on the image. You can also use any other standard Photoshop magnification techniques.

7 Workflow Options, along the bottom of the window, provide useful information on color space, file size, bit depth, and resolution. To change any of these settings, click the workflow link to display the Workflow Options dialog box.

Saving Camera Raw Images

1 When you are satisfied with your settings, you can click the Open Image button to open a copy of the Camera Raw file in Photoshop, if you want to do further work on it.

2 Click the Save Image button to save a copy of the Camera Raw file in JPEG, PSD, TIFF or DNG format.

Save Image...

3 Click the Done button to save the current settings with the original Camera Raw file, and close the Camera Raw dialog box.

Graduated Filter Tool

The Graduated Filter tool is an excellent example of the power and flexibility of working in Camera Raw format. It allows you to make selective, local adjustments on an image, and to simulate a traditional graduated neutral density filter, used by photographers to compensate for compositions with an extreme range of exposure requirements, such as the sky and the foreground in a landscape.

1 In the Camera Raw dialog box, click on the Graduated Filter tool to select it. The Graduated Filter controls appear on the right of the dialog box, below the Histogram, and the mask radio button is set to New.

2 Make a change to one of the controls – Exposure, for example – to select the type of adjustment for the filter. This setting is initially applied when you drag to define the area of the adjustment in the next step.

3 Drag in the image preview to define the area where you want to apply the adjustment. As you drag, the green dot and the dashed line represent the starting edge of the filter, the red dot and dashed line the end. Hold down Shift as you drag, to constrain the direction of the filter.

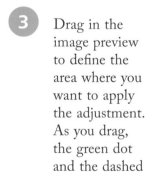

4 In the filter controls, the Edit radio button (○ New ◉ Edit) becomes active. Continue to create settings using the sliders, to achieve the results you require. Click either the Save Image, Open Image, Cancel or Done button when you are ready.

Hot tip

The Graduated Filter tool applies the settings you create across a gradient – the strength of the effect is greatest at the start of the filter gradient, and has minimal impact at the end – this creates the gradual transition, which blends the new settings into the image, keeping the adjustment realistic.

Hot tip

Click the Before/After button to see a split window showing the original and adjusted image. Continue to click the Before/After button to cycle through Before/After variations. Click and hold on the button to access views from the Before/After sub-menu.

Hot tip

Deselect the Show Overlay checkbox to preview the results without the filter guides.

Saving Files

The basic principles of saving files in Photoshop – using "Save" and "Save As" – are the same as in any other Macintosh or Windows application. Save regularly as you modify an image, so that you do not lose any changes you make should a system crash occur. You should use Save As to save a new file in the first instance, to make copies of a file, to save a file to a new location, and when you need to save an image in a different file format.

Photoshop supports numerous file formats for opening and saving images. Typically, you save an image in a particular format to meet specific output or printing specifications, to compress the image to save disk space, or to open or import the image into an application that requires a particular file format.

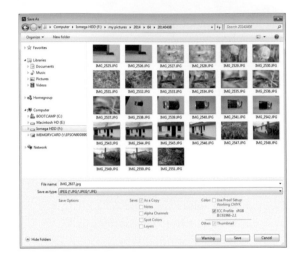

Hot tip

To create a thumbnail icon that displays in the Thumbnail area of the Open dialog box, choose Edit > Preferences > File Handling (Windows), or Photoshop > Preferences > File Handling (Mac). Select Always Save from the Image Previews pop-up:

Hot tip

In the File Saving Options area of File Handling preferences, leave the Save in Background option selected, so that when you save a file, you do not have to wait for the file to finish saving and you can continue working.

Hot tip

When you save an image with layers in Photoshop format, you get an option to Maximize Compatibility. For greatest flexibility in using the image in conjunction with other Adobe products, select this option, although this can increase the file size slightly.

1 To save an image in the first instance, choose File > Save As. Specify where you want to save the file. Enter a name for the file. Use the Format pop-up to choose an appropriate format. Click the Save button. File extensions are added automatically.

2 To save changes as you work on an image, choose File > Save. The previously-saved file information is updated.

Photoshop format

Use this format as you work on your image – all Photoshop options, in particular layers, remain available to you in this format. Photoshop also performs open and save routines more quickly when using its native format.

TIFF Format

TIFF (Tagged Image File Format) became a standard file format for scanned images in the early days of desktop publishing. It is common on both Mac and Windows platforms, and is compatible with most paint, image-editing, and page layout applications.

1 To save an image in TIFF format, choose File > Save As. The Save As dialog box appears. Specify where you want to save the image, and enter a name in the name entry box. Use the Format/Save as type pop-up menu to choose TIFF, then click Save.

| File name: | ny-eagle.psd |
| Format: | Photoshop (*.PSD;*.PDD) |

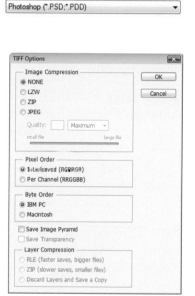

2 The TIFF Options dialog box appears. Select Image Compression, and other options as required, then click OK in the dialog box.

Pixel Order
Early versions of Photoshop wrote TIFFs with channel order interleaved. Per Channel usually produces better compression. Both are compatible with earlier versions of Photoshop.

Byte Order
Use this option to specify whether you want the TIFF to be used on a Mac or a PC, as Mac and PC TIFF formats vary slightly. Most recently-released applications can read files using either option.

LZW Compression
(Lempel-Zif-Welch) is a compression format that looks for repeated elements in the computer code that describes the image, and replaces these with shorter sequences. It is a

On the Macintosh, choose Photoshop > Preferences > File Handling, to specify whether or not you want file extensions – e.g. ".tif" – automatically added when saving files.

A warning appears at the bottom of the Save As dialog box if an image uses features, such as layers or alpha channels, that are not supported by that particular file format. You are prompted to save a copy of the file. Photoshop automatically adds the word "copy" to the file name.

...cont'd

"lossless" compression scheme – none of the image detail is lost. Applications such as QuarkXPress and Adobe InDesign can import TIFFs with LZW compression.

Zip

Zip is a lossless compression format, and achieves greatest compression in images that contain areas of solid color. Zip compression is supported by PDF and TIFF file formats.

JPEG

JPEG is a "lossy" compression format (see page 46). JPEG compression is most suitable for photographic-type images, with variations in highlight and shadow detail throughout the image. (See page 46 for further information on choosing quality options for JPEG compression.)

Save Image Pyramid

Although Photoshop itself cannot work with multiple resolutions in the same file, you can select the Save Image Pyramid option to preserve multiple resolutions already in a file. Some applications (such as Adobe InDesign) provide support for opening multiresolution files.

Save Transparency

For images that contain transparent areas, you can select Save Transparency. Transparent areas are saved in an additional Alpha channel, for use when the file is opened in a different application. Transparency is always retained when a file is opened in Photoshop.

Layer Compression

Photoshop can read layer information saved in TIFF file format, although most other applications cannot. Files saved with layers are larger than image files that have been flattened into a single layer. Choose Layer Compression options to specify how pixel data in layers is compressed. RLE (Run Length Encoding) is a lossless compression format supported by many Windows file formats. Select Discard Layers and Save a Copy, if you do not want to preserve layers in the image.

Hot tip

4 gigabytes is the maximum file size for TIFF images in Photoshop.

44

Hot tip

You can save images in CMYK, RGB, Lab, Index Color, and Grayscale, using TIFF file format.

Photoshop EPS

EPS generates file sizes that can be two to four times greater than TIFFs with LZW compression. To save in EPS format, do the following action.

1 Follow the procedure for saving TIFFs, but choose Photoshop EPS from the Format pop-up menu. Click OK. The EPS Options dialog box appears. Specify your settings, then click OK.

You can save Duotone, CMYK, RGB, Lab, Bitmap, and Grayscale images using Photoshop EPS file format.

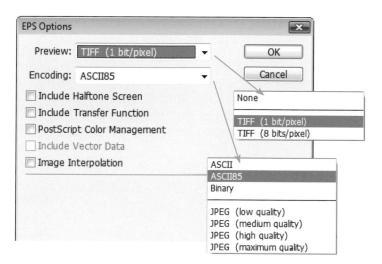

Preview

This option specifies the quality of the low-resolution screen preview you see when you import the image into applications, such as Adobe InDesign and QuarkXPress. Use "Macintosh (8-bits/pixel)" for a color preview. "Macintosh (JPEG)" uses JPEG compression routines, but is only supported by PostScript Level 2 or higher printers. Use TIFF if you want to use the image in Windows.

Encoding

The encoding option determines how image data is transmitted to the printing device. Use binary encoding if you want to export the image for use with Adobe Illustrator. Binary encoding typically produces a smaller file size. Some applications do not recognize binary encoding; in this case, you have to use ASCII. JPEG encoding options discard image data in order to create smaller file sizes.

Try choosing ASCII or ASCII85 if you experience printing problems, or network issues, with images saved in Photoshop EPS format.

Select the Include Vector Data checkbox to include vector data, such as shapes or type, present in the image.

Save As JPEG

JPEG is a compression format, widely used for preparing images for the World Wide Web as well as for print. Use JPEG when you are working with photographic-type images, and when preserving color detail and quality in the image is more important than download time considerations. JPEG does not allow transparency, and file sizes may be larger than for images exported in GIF format, depending on the compression level you choose.

Hot tip

Save images with gradients in the JPEG format, as this format typically produces smaller file sizes than GIFs with an Adaptive palette.

1 To save an image in JPEG format, choose File > Save As. Specify a location, enter a name, then choose JPEG from the Formats pop-up. Click OK in the dialog box.

2 Choose a color from the Matte pop-up to simulate background transparency in the image. You need to know the background color of the Web page in order to match the matte color to it.

3 Use the Quality pop-up to specify the amount of compression, or drag the slider. "Maximum" gives the best quality, retaining

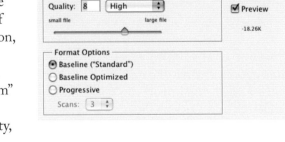

most of the detail in the image, but with the least compression. "Low" gives the lowest image quality, but maximum compression.

Don't forget

JPEG is most suited to compressing continuous-tone images (images in which the distinction between immediately neighboring pixels is slight). JPEG is not the best format for saving flat color images.

4 For Format Options, choose Baseline Optimized to optimize the color quality of the image. Select Progressive, and enter a number for Scans, to download the image in a series of passes that add detail progressively, until the image is completely displayed. Click OK to export the file.

Creating a New File

When you need a fresh, completely blank canvas to work on, you can create a new file.

1 To create a new file, choose File > New. Enter a name for the new document (or leave this as Untitled and do a Save As later).

Whilst the New dialog box is active, if you have images already open, you can select the name of any open file from the Preset pop-up menu; the New dialog box updates with the settings from the file you selected.

2 Specify your own Width and Height settings, or choose a category from the Preset menu, then specific dimensions from the Size pop-up. If you have copied pixels to the clipboard, the Preset menu is automatically set to Clipboard, and the Width and Height entry boxes reflect the dimensions of the elements on the clipboard.

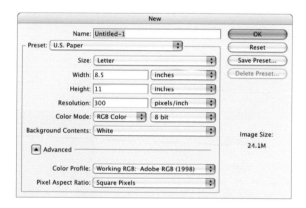

Photoshop creates a new file, with square pixels by default. Click the Advanced expand button (⊗), then use the Pixel Aspect Ratio drop down menu, to choose an aspect ratio other than square:

47

3 Enter a resolution, and choose a color mode. You can also specify whether you want to create a file with 1-, 8-, 16- or 32-bits per channel.

4 Select one of the Background Contents options to specify the canvas background you want to begin with, then click OK in the dialog box.

5 To change the color of the canvas after you click OK in the New dialog box, select a foreground color (see page 61). Next, choose Edit > Fill. Choose Foreground Color from the Use pop-up. Make sure Opacity is set to 100% and Mode is Normal. Click OK.

To specify a different Pixel Aspect Ratio for an existing image, choose View > Pixel Aspect Ratio. Select an aspect ratio from the sub-menu.

Photomerge

The Photomerge command automates the process of combining two or more images into a panoramic image. The Photomerge command arranges source images based on the overlapping content of each image, as well as blending the images to prevent obvious seams where lighting and exposure may vary.

Hot tip

Reposition allows Photoshop to match and align source images, but does not transform any image detail. Collage matches areas of overlapping content, and applies scaling and rotation if necessary.

48

1 Open the images you want to use for the photomerge composition. Choose File > Automate > Photomerge. In the Photomerge dialog box, click the Add Open Files button to import the images you want to merge. Make sure you select each image you want to merge. For the best results, leave the Blend Images Together checkbox selected, to allow Photoshop to color match images and produce a seamless blend along image borders.

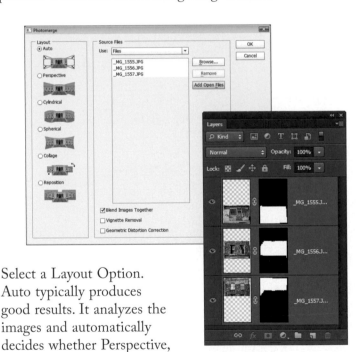

2 Select a Layout Option. Auto typically produces good results. It analyzes the images and automatically decides whether Perspective, Cylindrical or Spherical methods achieve the best result.

3 When you click OK, Photoshop arranges each source image on a separate layer in a new untitled_Panorama1 tab, using layer masks to blend images, where they overlap.

4 Image and Color Basics

This chapter covers a range of basic tasks – such as cropping an image and making it larger or smaller, or changing the resolution to suit your final output needs, – that you need to undertake on many of the images on which you work. Defining colors is another essential aspect of using Photoshop.

Rotating an Image

You can quickly rotate an image, if you have scanned it at the wrong orientation, or, for example, if you have imported an image in landscape orientation from a digital camera.

Hot tip

Choose Image > Image Rotation > Flip Canvas Horizontal/Vertical, to flip the entire image across its vertical or horizontal axis.

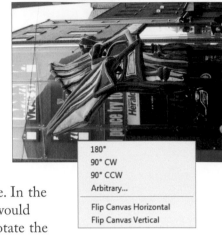

1 To rotate an image in set increments, use Image > Image Rotation. Choose one of the preset increments. CW stands for clockwise, CCW for counter-clockwise. In the example above, you would choose 90° CW to rotate the image upright.

Sometimes you need to adjust an image by a few degrees, to make up for a poor original photograph or slightly misaligned scan.

Hot tip

When using arbitrary rotation, position a ruler guide (see page 21, "Ruler Guides and Grids") to help determine how far you need to rotate:

2 To rotate in precise amounts, choose Image > Image Rotation > Arbitrary. Enter a value for the angle. Choose the CW or CCW radio button, then click OK in the dialog box.

3 You may need to recrop the image. Use the Smart Sharpen, or Unsharp Mask, filters to compensate for any blurring due to the rotation.

Resizing without Resampling

When you resize an image without resampling, you make the image larger or smaller without changing the total number of pixels in the image. The overall dimensions of the image change, the file size remains the same, but the resolution of the image goes up, if you make the image smaller, or down if you make the image larger.

Beware

When you make the image smaller, without resampling, the pixels get smaller. Effectively, you are increasing the resolution of the image. When you make an image bigger, without resampling, the pixels get larger, and this can lead to jagged, blocky results. Effectively, you are reducing the resolution of the image.

1 To decrease the size of your image, without resampling, choose Image > Image Size. Make sure that Resample is deselected. Enter a lower value in the Width or Height entry boxes, or enter a higher resolution. The other measurements update automatically. The file size of the image remains the same – no pixels were added. The resolution has increased – the same number of pixels are packed into a smaller area.

2 To increase the size of your image, without resampling, enter a higher value in the Width or Height entry box, or enter a lower resolution. The file size of the image remains the same, but the resolution has decreased.

Smaller without resampling

Original

Larger without resampling

As far as possible, try to avoid resampling up. You are adding pixels to the image without increasing the quality and detail in the image. When scanning an image, you get better results if you scan the image at the size at which you intend to use it, and at the resolution required for final output. When using a digital camera, make sure you set a high enough quality setting to capture sufficient image detail for your intended output.

When you are working in the Image Size dialog box, after making changes, to reset the dialog box values to their initial settings, hold down Alt/option on the keyboard. The Cancel button becomes a Reset button. Click the Reset button.

You can use this technique in other Photoshop dialog boxes as well.

Resampling Up

Resampling up involves interpolation. Interpolation is used when Photoshop has to add information – new pixels – that didn't previously exist in an image. Choose an interpolation option from the pop-up in the Image Size dialog box. Preserve Details (enlargement) gives the best results when you need to increase the size or resolution of an image, but takes the longest. Nearest Neighbor is the quickest, but least accurate. Bilinear gives a medium quality result. Bicubic Smoother is based on Bicubic; it is intended for enlarging images, and can produce smoother results. Bicubic Sharper is useful for reducing the size of images, when preparing them for the Web. Select Automatic to allow Photoshop to select the best option depending on its analysis of the image content.

Automatic	Alt+1
Preserve Details (enlargement)	Alt+2
Bicubic Smoother (enlargement)	Alt+3
Bicubic Sharper (reduction)	Alt+4
Bicubic (smooth gradients)	Alt+5
Nearest Neighbor (hard edges)	Alt+6
Bilinear	Alt+7

When you resample up, new pixels are added to the image, so the file size increases. Resampling takes place when you increase the resolution setting, or the Width/Height settings with the Resample option selected. This example starts with a 2 inches by 2 inches image at 150 ppi.

1 Choose Image > Image Size. To keep the overall dimensions of the image, but increase

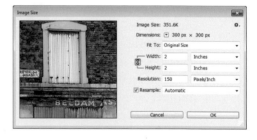

the resolution, make sure that Resample is selected. Make sure the Constrain Aspect Ratio link icon (🔗) is active, so that the image's original proportions are maintained. Enter a higher value in the Resolution box.

2 The file size, and total number of pixels, increase, but the Width and Height settings remain the same.

You now have an image that is the same overall size, but which has more pixels in the same area, and, therefore, its resolution is increased.

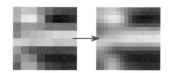

Beware

When you resample an image, blurring may occur due to the process of interpolation. You can use the Smart Sharpen or Unsharp Mask filters to partially compensate for this (see pages 195-197).

3 To make the overall dimensions of the image bigger, but to keep the same resolution, again make sure that

Resample is selected. Make sure the Constrain Aspect Ratio link icon (🔲) is active, to keep width and height proportional. Enter a higher value in either the Width or Height entry boxes. (The other entry box updates automatically, when the Constrain Aspect Ration link icon is active.)

4 The overall dimensions of the image have now increased. The file size and total number of pixels have also increased, but the resolution remains the same.

Sampling Down

You sometimes need to resample down, to maintain an optimal balance between the resolution needed for acceptable final output and file size considerations. There is little point in working with an image at too high a resolution, if some of the image information is redundant at final output.

Resampling down means discarding pixels. The result is a smaller file size. Resampling down occurs when you decrease the resolution setting, or the Width/Height settings with the Resample option selected.

These examples start with a 2 inches by 2 inches image at 300 ppi.

Hot tip

Choose View > Print Size, to get a representation on screen of the physical size of the image when printed.

1 Choose Image > Image Size. To keep the overall dimensions of the image,

but decrease the resolution, make sure that Resample is selected. Make sure the Constrain Aspect Ratio link icon (⬚) is active, so that the image's original proportions are maintained. Reduce the value in the Resolution box.

Hot tip

Click the Constrain Aspect Ratio button to toggle it off (⬚) and on (⬚).

2 The file size goes down, and the total number of pixels decreases, whilst the Width and Height settings remain the same.

You now have an image that is the same overall size, but with fewer pixels in the same area, and, therefore, its resolution is lower.

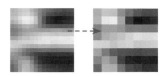

③ To reduce the overall dimensions of the image, but keep the image at the same resolution, make sure that Resample is selected. Make sure the Constrain Aspect Ratio link icon () is active, to keep the width and height proportional. Enter a lower value in either the Width or Height entry box. (The other entry box updates automatically, when the Constrain Aspect Ration link icon is active.)

④ The overall dimensions of the image have now decreased. The file size and the total number of pixels have also decreased, but the resolution remains the same.

 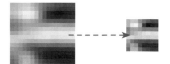

Cropping an Image

Use the Crop tool to define the area of an image that you want to use as your composition. You can choose whether to delete pixels outside the crop area (and reduce the file size), or retain them, without them being visible, so that you can recompose the crop at a later stage if necessary.

Hot tip

Use the Crop Options pop-up in the Options bar to hide/show the crop shading overlay. You can also change the color and/or opacity of the crop shading:

Hot tip

Use the Delete Cropped Pixels checkbox in the Options bar to specify whether pixels outside the crop area are retained or deleted. If you retain cropped pixels, to recrop the image at a later stage, select the crop tool, then click inside the crop area to reveal the original image pixels.

When cropping, the Rule Of Thirds overlay is on by default. It helps you compose the crop to pleasing proportions. You can choose alternative crop overlays or switch them off using the View pop-up in the Options bar.

1 Select the Crop tool. Crop handles appear on the boundary of the image. Position your cursor on any of the crop handles. When the cursor changes to a bi-directional arrow, click and drag to define the crop area. The crop area automatically centers in the

Photoshop window as you drag. The area of the image outside the crop dims, to indicate the parts of the image to be discarded. Alternatively, with the Crop tool selected, position your cursor within the image, then click and drag to define the crop area.

2 To reposition the crop, place your cursor inside the crop area, then click and drag. To resize the crop, place your cursor on one of the eight crop handles around the crop area (the cursor changes to a bi-directional arrow), then click and drag. To rotate, position your cursor just outside the crop area (the cursor changes shape to indicate rotation –), then click and drag in a circular direction.

3 To straighten an image as you crop it, click the Straighten tool in the Options bar. Click and drag across the image to indicate the correct vertical or horizontal plane.

4 Click the Commit button in the Options bar, or press Return/Enter to crop the image. The areas outside the crop are discarded. Click the Cancel button, or press the Esc key if you want to remove the crop area without cropping.

Preserve Details Enlargement

When you resample an image – either, keeping the image the same size, but increasing the resolution, or increasing the size of the image whilst keeping the same resolution – Photoshop has to add pixels to the image that were not in the original image as captured. To add pixels Photoshop uses sophisticated computer algorithms to intelligently guess the color values for the pixels it adds. The Preserve Details Enlargement "interpolation" method provides the best results when you want to make an image larger and/or increase the resolution of an image.

Hot tip

Noise is the appearance of clusters of unwanted, visually intrusive pixels that add undesirable detail to an image. Use the Reduce Noise slider to reduce the amount of noise that can appear in an image as you resample up. Be careful not to overdo the reduce noise setting as this can lead to loss of detail in areas where you want to retain it.

1 To increase the size of the image and maintain the same resolution, choose Image > Image Size. In the Image Size dialog box, make sure the Resample checkbox is selected. Select Preserve Details (enlargement) from the Resample pop-up menu. Enter a higher width or height value.

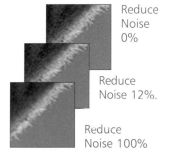

Reduce Noise 0%

Reduce Noise 12%.

Reduce Noise 100%

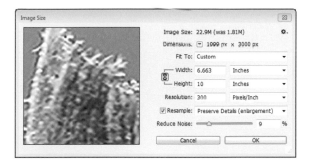

2 Use the Reduce Noise slider, or enter a value in the entry box to control the amount of noise, if required.

3 To keep an image at the same size, but increase its resolution, make sure that the Resample checkbox is selected, then enter a new value in the Resolution entry box.

Original: 6in x 4in at 300ppi. Scaled on page to 40%.

Detail of original enlarged to 10in x 6in at 300ppi. Scaled on page to 40%.

Adding a Border

Borders are useful when you need additional space around the edges of your image.

Hot tip

Select the Relative checkbox, then enter a positive or negative number, to specify the amount you want to either add to or subtract from the canvas size.

1 Choose Image > Canvas Size. Use the measurement pop-up menus, to choose a unit of measurement. Enter increased values for the Width and/or Height fields.

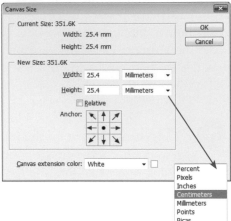

2 To specify where the border is added, relative to the image, click one of the placement squares. This sets the relative position of the image and the border. The highlight square (▪) represents the position of the image, the other squares the position of the border.

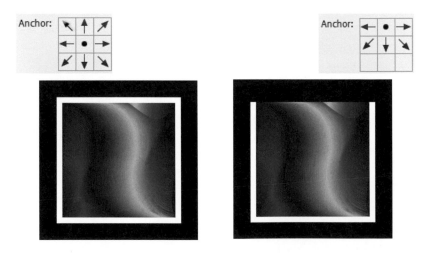

3 Choose a color from the Canvas extension color pop-up menu, to specify the color of the border. Click OK in the dialog to add the border. This increases the file size, as the command adds pixels to the image.

Image Modes

Image modes are fundamental to working in Photoshop. When you open an image, the mode is indicated in the title bar of the image window. There are eight different modes in Photoshop. Use modes as appropriate to your working requirements. Then, depending on output or printing requirements, if necessary, convert to a different mode.

RGB mode
Images are typically scanned or captured in RGB mode. When you start work with a color image, it is usually best to work in RGB mode, as this is faster than CMYK mode, and allows you to use all of Photoshop's commands and features, providing greatest flexibility.

The disadvantage of working in RGB mode, if your image will be printed commercially on a printing press, is that RGB allows a greater gamut of colors than you can print. At some stage, some of the brightest, more vibrant colors may lose their brilliance, when the image is brought within the CMYK gamut of the press.

CMYK mode
Convert to CMYK when the image is to be printed commercially, and you have finished making changes.

To place a color image in a page layout application, from where it will be color separated, you need to convert from RGB to CMYK. When you convert from RGB to CMYK, Photoshop adjusts any colors in the RGB image that fall outside the CMYK gamut, to their nearest printable color. (See page 63 for details on gamut warnings.)

You can also select View > Gamut Warning (Ctrl/Command + Shift + Y), to highlight (in gray) pixels in the image that are out of gamut.

Indexed Color mode
This mode reduces your image to 256 colors or less, and is used frequently for multimedia and Web images.

Duotone
Duotone is a popular effect used to give added tonal depth to a grayscale image, by printing with black and another color. Save duotones in EPS or PDF file format so that they color-separate correctly from page layout applications.

To retain the flexibility of working in RGB mode, but to see an on-screen CMYK preview of your image, first make sure that View > Proof Setup is set to Working CMYK, then choose View > Proof Colors. The title bar of the image changes, to indicate that you are working with an RGB image, but previewing in CMYK:

bedlamasbestos_2x2_150.tif @ 100% (RGB/8*/CMYK) ×

You must first convert to Grayscale mode before you can convert to Bitmap or Duotone mode.

To achieve greater creative flexibility when converting an image to grayscale, choose Image > Adjustments > Black & White. (See page 191 for further information.)

...cont'd

Grayscale mode
When you are not printing an image in color, you can convert to Grayscale mode to make work faster and file size smaller.

Lab mode
This mode uses the CIE Lab model, which has one channel for luminosity, an "a" channel representing colors blue to yellow, and a "b" channel for magenta to green. A significant advantage to this mode is that its gamut encompasses that of both CMYK and RGB modes.

Bitmap mode
This mode reduces everything to black or white pixels. The image becomes a 1-bit image.

Multichannel mode
Multichannel mode uses 256 levels of gray in each channel. When you convert RGB or CMYK images to multichannel mode, the original channels in the image are converted to spot color channels. Multichannel mode is an advanced option – only use it if you have a detailed understanding of the printing process.

1 To convert from one mode to another, choose Image > Mode, then choose the mode you want from the sub-menu. Depending on which mode you are converting from and to, you may get a message box warning you of any consequences of converting to the new mode, and asking you to confirm your request.

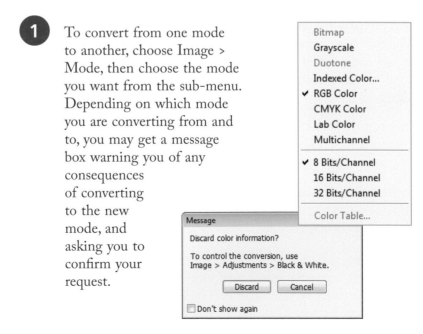

Foreground & Background Colors

The foreground color is applied when you first create type, and when you use the Paint Bucket, Line, Pencil, and Brush tools.

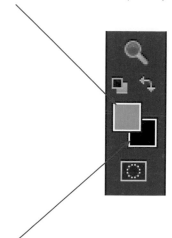

Hot tip

Press X on the keyboard to switch background and foreground colors. Press D on the keyboard to revert to the default foreground and background colors.

The background color is the color you get when you delete or move a selection on the Background layer, or when you use the Eraser tool on the Background layer.

When you are working with foreground and background controls, you can also switch colors, and you can quickly change back to the default colors, black and white.

You can change the background and foreground colors using the Eyedropper tool, the Color Picker dialog box, the Color panel, and the Swatches panel.

1 To switch background to foreground, and vice versa, click once on the Switch Colors arrow.

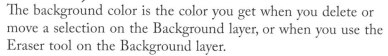

2 To revert to black and white as the default background and foreground colors, click the Default Colors icon.

Eyedropper and Color Sampler

The Eyedropper tool

The Eyedropper tool provides a quick and convenient way to pick up foreground and

background color, from an area of the image you are working on, or from another inactive Photoshop image window.

Hot tip

Use the Sample pop-up menu in the Options bar to specify which layers the Eyedropper tool samples color from:

1 To set the foreground color, click on the Eyedropper tool. Position your cursor, then click once on the image. The Set foreground color box in the Tool panel now represents the color where you clicked.

2 To set the background color, hold down Alt/option, then click on the image. The Set background color box in the Tool panel now indicates the color on which you clicked.

3 To set the Sample Size, use the Sample Size pop-up menu in the Options bar to choose a value. Point Sample reads the precise value of the pixel on which you click – 3 by 3 Average, etc. takes average values of the pixels where you click.

Hot tip

To hide/show the sample points, choose Color Samplers from the Info panel menu.

Hot tip

With the Color Sampler tool selected, you can click the Clear All button in the options bar to quickly delete all sample points in an image.

The Color Sampler tool

Use the Color Sampler tool (with the Info panel) to set up to 10 sample points, which you can refer to as you make adjustments to color values. Each time you click in the image window with the Color Sampler tool, you set a sample point. Each point creates an extra pane in the Info panel. To delete a sample point, drag it out of the image window with the Color Sampler tool.

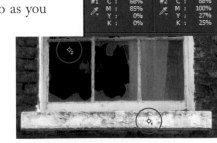

The Color Picker

Using the Color Picker is a powerful and flexible way of choosing foreground and background colors. You can use a number of different color models to create color.

1 To create a Process color, using the Color Picker, click once on either the Set foreground or Set background color box. Enter values in the CMYK

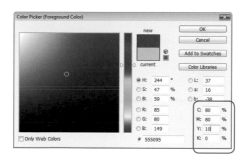

entry boxes. A preview of the color appears in the new color swatch, above the current color swatch.

2 Click OK on the dialog box. The color you defined now becomes the foreground or background color, depending on which box you clicked in Step 1.

You can also create colors, using the Color Slider and the Color Field. The next example uses Hue, Saturation and Brightness values. Use the same techniques for RGB and Lab color models.

1 To create a color using Hue, Saturation and Brightness (HSB) values, first click the Hue (H) radio button.

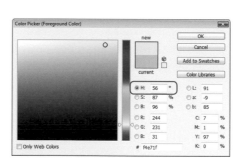

2 Click on the Color Slider bar, or drag the slider triangles on either side of the bar, to choose a hue or color. This sets one of the three HSB values. The number in the Hue entry box represents the hue you have chosen.

Hot tip

Press the Tab key to move the highlight through the entry boxes in the dialog box.

Beware

A warning triangle – the Gamut alarm – appears next to the new/current color boxes, if you create a color that cannot be printed using CMYK inks. Click the warning triangle to choose the nearest printable color:

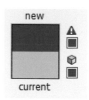

The small box below the warning triangle indicates the nearest printable color.

...cont'd

To create a Web-safe color, select the Only Web Colors option. The Web palette consists of 216 colors:

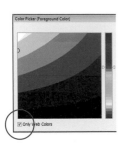

3 Next, click in the Color Field to set the other two variables – Saturation and Brightness. Clicking to the left of the field reduces the saturation, clicking to the right increases the saturation of the selected hue. Clicking near the bottom decreases brightness, clicking near the top increases brightness for the selected hue.

4 If you click on the Saturation button, the Color Slider now represents saturation (from 0-100), and the Color Field allows you to choose Hue and Brightness values. When you click the Brightness radio button, the slider represents Brightness, and the Color Field represents Hue and Saturation.

If the Only Web Colors option is deselected, the Non-Web Color alert appears, if you create a color that is not in the Web palette. Click the Web alert icon to move the color to the nearest Web-safe color:

Choosing Custom Colors

You can access a range of color-matching systems, such as PANTONE, Toyo Color Finder, and Focoltone Color System, using the Color Libraries dialog box.

1 In the Color Picker dialog box, click the Color Libraries button. Use the Book pop-up menu to select a color-matching system.

2 If you know the ink number of the color you want, you can enter the number on the keyboard. Alternatively, click in the color slider bar to the right of the ink color boxes. This moves you to a general range of colors. Use the scroll bars at the top and bottom of the sliders to find the specific color you want. Click on the color you want to select, then click OK.

In the Color Libraries dialog box, click the Picker button to return to the Color Picker dialog box.

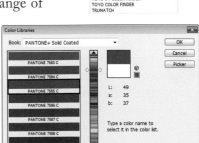

The Color Panel

You can also use the Color panel (Window > Color) to mix new colors.

1 First, identify which color selection box is "active". There are two boxes; Set foreground color and Set background color. The active box is outlined in black.

2 Continue with step 3, if the correct box is active, or click the inactive box to make it the active box, if necessary.

3 Drag the Color slider triangle ( ) on the Hue ramp on the right side of the panel to specify the color range. Then, click in the color cube, or drag the target circle, to set brightness and saturation values.

4 Use the panel menu button ( ), in the top right of the panel, to change the color model controls for the panel.

5 Position your cursor on the bottom, left or right edge of the panel, then click and drag to resize the panel as required.

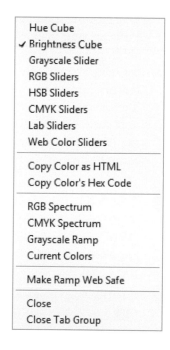

Hue Cube
✓ Brightness Cube
Grayscale Slider
RGB Sliders
HSB Sliders
CMYK Sliders
Lab Sliders
Web Color Sliders

Copy Color as HTML
Copy Color's Hex Code

RGB Spectrum
CMYK Spectrum
Grayscale Ramp
Current Colors

Make Ramp Web Safe

Close
Close Tab Group

Hot tip

Click the active color selection box to display the Color Picker dialog.

Beware

During step 3, if you create a color that is outside the CMYK color gamut, the gamut alert warning triangle appears. You can click on the alert triangle to set the color to the nearest CMYK equivalent. The nearest CMYK equivalent appears in a box next to the alert triangle:

Hot tip

Choose RGB Sliders from the panel menu if you want the Color panel to appear as it did in previous versions of Photoshop.

The Swatches Panel

You can use the Swatches panel (Window > Swatches) to set foreground and background colors, and you can also use it to create custom color palettes, which you can save and then reload into a different image. The Swatches panel is also one of the default panels in the Essentials workspace.

See page 27 for details on loading and saving custom panel settings.

Hot tip

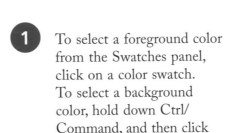

1 To select a foreground color from the Swatches panel, click on a color swatch. To select a background color, hold down Ctrl/ Command, and then click on a color swatch.

You can customize the Swatches panel by adding and deleting colors in the panel.

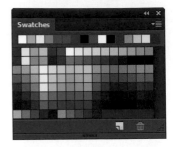

Hot tip

The top row of color boxes in the Swatches panel records the 16 most recently sampled colors. Choose Show Recent Colors from the Swatches panel menu to hide/show this row:

2 To add color to the swatches, select a foreground color. Position your cursor in an empty area of the Swatches panel. (The cursor changes to a paint bucket.) Then click. Enter a name for the new swatch, then click OK to add the current foreground color to the Swatches panel.

3 To delete a color swatch, hold down Alt/option (Mac) or Alt (Windows), and then click on a color swatch.

Hot tip

Position your cursor on a swatch, in the Swatches panel, hold down Ctrl (Mac) then click the mouse button, or click the right mouse button (PC), to access the context sensitive menu:

4 Use the Swatches panel menu ( ) to reset the Swatches panel to its default settings, or to choose a different color palette from the list.

5 The Painting Tools

The painting tools apply color to pixels in an image, and can also be used for editing masks. The Brush Preset Picker, the Brush panel, and controls available in the Options bar, allow you to control all aspects of painting.

The Brush Preset Picker

The Brush Preset Picker in the Options bar allows quick, convenient access to a range of standard, preset brushes.

Don't forget

Rest your cursor on the brush thumbnail, in the Brush Preset scroll box, to see a descriptive help label for the tool:

1 To select a brush, click on the Brush tool to select it, then click the Brush Preset picker pop-up triangle in the Options bar.

2 Click on a brush you want to use, in the scroll box. A thumbnail icon represents the shape of the brush. The number beneath the brush icon indicates the diameter of the brush, in pixels.

Hot tip

For circular shape brushes, use the Hardness slider to increase/decrease the hardness setting for the edge of the brush (see page 74 for further information on setting Hardness).

3 To change the size of the brush, drag the Size slider to increase/decrease the size of the brush, or enter a value in pixels, in the size entry box. Click the Restore to original size button (🔄) to return to the original size of the brush, if you have made changes to the size. (This option is only available for brush tip shapes created originally from a sample of pixels.)

4 Create settings for Mode, Opacity and Flow, in the Options bar, and choose the Airbrush build-up option, if required.

Hot tip

For a description of blending modes, see pages 81-83.

5 Position your cursor in the image window, then click and drag to apply the foreground color, using the current brush characteristics and the brush settings in the Options bar.

Opacity

Opacity (Brush, Pencil, History Brush, Art History Brush, Gradient, Paint Bucket, Clone Stamp, and Pattern Stamp tools) controls how "completely" pixels are covered with the foreground color, when you drag across them.

Make sure the Opacity slider is at 100%, if you want to completely cover the pixels you drag across. (Soft-edged brushes only partially cover pixels around the edge of the painting stroke, to create the soft edge effect.) Reducing the Opacity setting gives less complete results in the area you drag across, creating a semi-transparent, partially-covered effect.

100%

60%

20%

Flow

Flow controls how quickly paint is applied when you drag the brush across the image.

100%

60%

20%

Airbrush build-up

Select the Airbrush build-up option to imitate the effect of spraying paint with an airbrush. The Airbrush option works best with soft-edged brushes, and reduced Opacity and Flow settings.

Brush: 90p x Soft Edge
Opacity: 80%
Flow: 40%

Remember to choose the foreground color you want to paint with, before you start to use a painting tool.

(Windows) Hold down Alt, then right-click and drag left to decrease, right to increase the size of the painting tool cursor. (Mac) Hold down Ctrl + Alt/option, then drag left or right. Use the same techniques as above, but drag down to reduce brush opacity, up to increase brush opacity.

The Airbrush build-up option is selected when the icon in the Options bar has a dark background:

69

The Brush Panel

The Brush panel provides access to a wide variety of options, for controlling the appearance and characteristics of your brush strokes. You can alter the characteristics of preset brushes, or you can create your own custom brushes, using a variety of interchangeable settings.

If the Brush panel appears dimmed, you do not have an appropriate Painting or Editing tool selected.

1 To create custom brush characteristics, select a painting tool. Choose Window > Brush (F5) to show the Brush panel, if it is not already showing.

2 Click on a preset brush in the scroll list on the right of the Brush panel. Any settings you create in the left hand column remain selected when you choose a different brush preset.

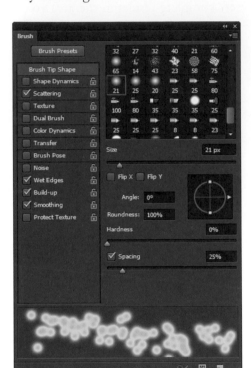

If you use a pressure sensitive graphics drawing tablet, you can select the Always use Pressure for Opacity ( ) and Always use Pressure for Size ( ) buttons, in the Options bar, to override opacity and size settings in the Brush panel.

3 To customize the selected preset brush, by adding your own brush settings, click the checkboxes ( ) to the left of the brush characteristic labels. The preview pane at the bottom of the panel updates to indicate the effect on the brush. (In this example, the 21-pixel, soft-edged brush is selected, with Scattering, Smoothing, Build Up and Wet Edges also applied.)

You can also use the Brush panel for setting the brush characteristics for Editing tools (see Chapter 6).

4 Drag the Size slider to change the diameter of the brush, or enter a value, in pixels, in the entry box.

5 Change shape settings, such as Angle, Roundness, Hardness and Spacing, if required (see page 74 for further information).

6 Click the brush characteristic label (to the right of the check box) to access a range of controls for the option. (See page 72 for information on creating custom brush characteristic settings.) Click Brush Tip Shape to return the display, on the right of the dialog box, to the Brush Presets picker scroll box.

Selecting the Airbrush build-up option in the Options panel, is the equivalent of selecting Build-up from the effects list in the Brushes panel.

7 Create settings for Mode, Opacity, and Flow in the Options bar.

8 If you click on a different brush in the scroll list, custom brush characteristic settings for the previously selected brush are retained. Create a tool preset, if you want to save the settings on a permanent basis (see page 75 for further information).

Use the Brush Presets Picker panel in the Options bar (see pages 68-69) when you want to quickly select a brush from the existing set of brushes. Use the Brush panel to select a preset brush, and then to create and design your own custom brushes.

9 Position your cursor in the image window, then click and drag to create the required paint stroke.

Custom Brush Settings

Preset brushes can be customized using the style options on the left side of the Brushes panel, together with the settings that control the Brush Tip Shape. The first seven effects (between divider bars) have controls that allow you to customize each effect. The last five style options cannot be edited.

To understand what Photoshop refers to as paint marks, in the Brush panel select a simple preset brush, click the Brush Tip Shape button, then drag the spacing slider to the right.

The Preview box indicates, visually, how the individual paint marks form a paint stroke when you drag the Brush tool in the image window.

1 To create custom settings for a brush effect, such as Shape Dynamics, click the effect label (the words "Shape Dynamics") – not the checkbox. The controls available for each brush effect appear on the right of the dialog box.

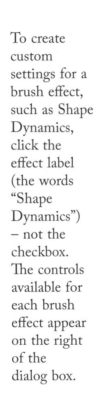

2 Experiment with the available settings. The preview box, at the bottom of the panel, updates to reflect changes you make to the settings.

Shape Dynamics

The Shape Dynamics options control the manner in which brush marks in the painting stroke change as you drag your cursor in the image window.

Scattering

Scattering settings allow you to specify how the position of the paint marks in a stroke is varied, and also control the number of paint marks in a stroke.

To constrain your painting strokes to straight lines, click with the Painting tool. To position the start of the stroke, move your cursor (do not click and drag), then hold down Shift and click to end the stroke.

Texture
Use texture settings on a brush to associate the brush with a pattern, to create paint strokes that appear to be painted on a textured canvas.

Dual Brush
Dual Brush uses two tips to create the brush stroke. Set options for the primary tip, using options in the Brush Tip Shape area. Set options for the secondary tip in the Dual Brush area.

Color Dynamics
Color Dynamics settings control how the color of the painting stroke varies over the length of the stroke.

Transfer
Transfer controls determine the degree of variation in the speed with which paint is applied, and also the opacity of the paint in the stroke.

Brush Pose
Use Brush Pose settings to control tilt angle as well as rotation and pressure for the brush tip.

Noise
Noise has the most apparent effect around the edges of soft-edged brushes, and creates a random scattering of pixels.

Wet Edges
Wet Edges creates a stroke that is darker around the edges and translucent inside the stroke, imitating the uneven build up of paint in a watercolor.

Build-up
The Build-up option on a soft-edged brush, with a medium-to-low Opacity setting, simulates the effect of spraying paint with an airbrush.

Smoothing
Smoothing helps create smoother curves in brush strokes.

Protect Texture
Select the Protect Texture option to keep texture effects consistent, when painting with different textured brush tips. The option applies the same pattern and scale to all preset brushes with a texture.

Brush Tip Shape Settings

The Brush Tip Shape options area of the Brush panel provides further controls for specifying the appearance of a brush stroke.

Hot tip

Bristle brushes have their own set of brush tip options, in the Brush panel. Experiment with the Bristle Qualities settings to create varied and interesting brush strokes. The Stiffness setting is useful if you are using a mouse to paint in the image:

 To create custom brush tip shape settings for a brush, first select a brush from the Brush Presets list. Make sure Brush Tip Shape is selected. Enter values for Size, Hardness, Flip, Spacing, Angle, and Roundness.

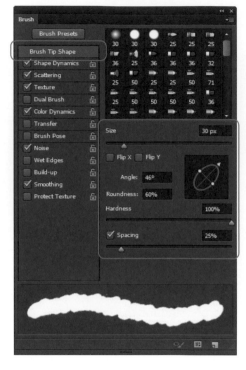

Size
Enter a value, in pixels, for the diameter of your brush, from 1-5000.

Hardness
A setting of 100% gives a hard-edged brush.
Lower settings produce soft-edged brushes. The lower you take this setting, the more diffuse the resultant stroke, when you paint with the brush. Even with settings of 100%, the edge of the brush stroke is anti-aliased.

Hot tip

To save custom brush tip settings for future use, see page 75 – "Brush Presets".

Spacing
Spacing is measured as a percentage of brush size. 25% is the default setting for standard round brushes. Higher settings begin to create non-continuous strokes.

Angle and Roundness
Use these controls together to create a stroke which thickens and thins like a calligraphic pen. You can enter values in the entry boxes, or drag the arrow indicator to change the angle, and drag the diameter dots to change the diameter.

Hot tip

Select the Flip X or Flip Y checkbox to flip the paint mark across its vertical or horizontal axis, to change the direction of the brush effect.

Brush Presets

Create a Brush preset when you have created custom brush settings that you want to be able to reuse, without first having to recreate the custom settings.

1 To create a Brush preset, select the Brush tool, then use the Brush panel to create custom settings for the brush.

2 In the Brush panel, from the panel menu ( ), choose New Brush Preset.

New Brush Preset...

Clear Brush Controls
Reset All Locked Settings
Copy Texture to Other Tools

Close
Close Tab Group

3 In the Brush Name dialog box enter a name. Click OK. The new Brush Preset is now available in the Brush Presets panel and in the Brush Presets Picker panel.

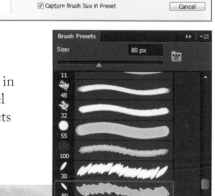

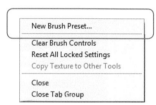

A Brush Preset allows you to save custom brush settings, so that you can access them quickly and easily whenever you need to, without having to first recreate the settings.

Mixer Brush Tool

The Mixer Brush tool allows you to blend painting colors on the brush with underlying colors in the image as you drag across them in a variety of ways, creating realistic painting effects. Using the Mixer Brush tool you can use mixed colors on the brush with the ability to vary the dynamics of the painting effect, including wetness and mixing, to achieve interesting and varied results.

You can click the Toggle Brush Panel button, in the Options bar, to Show/Hide the Brush panel:

1 Select the Mixer Brush tool from the Brush tool group.

2 Select a brush from the Brush Preset picker panel in the Options bar, or from the Brush Presets panel. Bristle tip brushes work well with the Mixer Brush tool.

3 Edit bristle qualities in the Brush panel, if required (see pages 72-73 for information on creating custom brush settings).

Select Load Solid Colors only from the Current Brush Load pop-up menu, if you want to sample solid color to the Current Brush Load color box, when you Alt/option click within the image:

4 To set the Current Brush Load color to a solid color, select a Foreground color (see page 61 for information on setting the Foreground color). To set mixed colors as the Current Brush Load color, position your cursor in the image, hold down Alt/option, then click to sample colors around the point where you click.

5 Use the Load brush after each stroke and the Clean brush after each stroke toggles to further control the behavior of the brush. Leave the Load brush button selected to reload the brush with the Current Brush Load color after you complete a paint stroke in the image. Switch it off, and the brush will not load with color – when you drag in the image, the brush mixes existing pixel colors only. Leave the Clean brush button switched on, so that colors from the previous paint stroke are not added to the colors on the brush for the next stroke. Switch it off when you want colors from the previous stroke to remain on the brush for the next stroke.

Hot tip

Click the Toggle Live Brush Tip Preview button ( ), at the bottom of the Brush Presets panel, to Show/ Hide a brush head preview in the top left corner of the Photoshop window:

6 Create settings for Wet, Load, Mix, and Flow.

Wet: 80% ▼ Load: 75% ▼ Mix: 90% ▼ Flow: 100% ▼ ⌇ ☐ Sample All Layers

7 Drag to create paint strokes in the image.

Wet
Wet sets the wetness of the pixels already in the image, not the wetness of the brush, and controls how much paint the brush picks up from the canvas.

Wet = 80%

Wet = 5%

Hot tip

The Presets pop-up menu provides a useful choice of Mixer Brush settings, which you can use as a starting point as you begin to experiment with the Mixer Brush tool:

Load
Load controls the amount of paint loaded to the brush. Higher settings allow longer strokes; paint runs out more quickly at lower settings.

Load = 90%

Load = 5%

Mix
Mix specifies the amount of paint used from the Current Brush Load, relative to the amount of paint from the canvas. Low Mix setting values apply more of the Current Brush Load color.

Mix = 90%

Mix = 5%

Flow
Flow controls how quickly paint is applied when you drag the brush across the image.

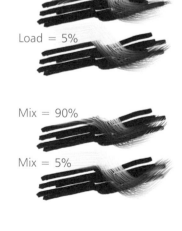

Wet, Heavy Mix	↕
Custom	
Dry	
Dry, Light Load	
Dry, Heavy Load	
Moist	
Moist, Light Mix	
Moist, Heavy Mix	
Wet	
Wet, Light Mix	
Wet, Heavy Mix	
Very Wet	
Very Wet, Light Mix	
Very Wet, Heavy Mix	

The Pencil Tool

You can use the Pencil tool to draw freeform lines. The lines you draw with the Pencil tool are always hard-edged – in other words, the edges of your lines are not anti-aliased. The Pencil tool paints or draws with the foreground color.

1 To draw a line, first select the Pencil tool. Set a brush size, using the Brush Preset Picker (see page 68). Or use the Brush panel to create custom brush settings for the tool (see page 70).

2 Use the Pencil Options bar to specify a blending mode from the Mode pop-up menu, Opacity, and Auto Erase options.

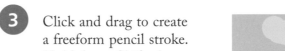

Hot tip

Hold down the Shift key then drag to constrain any brush stroke to vertical or horizontal. Click back on the painting tool if you want to create another, separate paint stroke using this technique.

3 Click and drag to create a freeform pencil stroke. Hold down Shift, then drag, to constrain the pencil stroke vertically or horizontally.

4 To create a straight pencil stroke between two points, click, move the cursor to a new position (do not click and drag), hold down Shift, then click again.

Auto Erase
Select this checkbox to use the Pencil tool to paint out or erase areas of foreground color, using the current background color.

The Gradient Tool

You can use the Gradient tool to create transitions from one color to another. You can also create multicolored gradients. There are options for Linear, Radial, Angle, Reflected, and Diamond gradients. You can apply a gradient fill to a selection, or to an entire active layer.

The default gradient uses the current Foreground and Background colours to form the gradient.

1 To create a gradient fill, select the Gradient tool. Choose a gradient type from the Options bar.

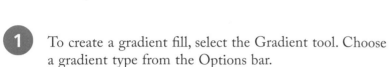

2 Select a blending mode from the Mode pop-up and set Opacity. Use the Gradient pop-up to choose one of the preset gradients.

Hold down Shift as you click and drag, to constrain a linear gradient to 45° increments.

3 Position your cursor where you want the gradient to start, then click and drag. The angle and distance you drag the cursor defines the angle and distance of a linear gradient, or the radius of a radial gradient. (Click and drag from the center out to create Radial, Angle, Reflected, and Diamond gradient fills.)

4 For basic gradient fills, you can leave the Transparency and Dither options selected. Choose the Reverse option to reverse the order of colors in the gradient.

For a linear gradient, the start and end colors fill any part of the selection or layer that you do not drag the cursor across. For radial gradients, the end color fills the remaining area.

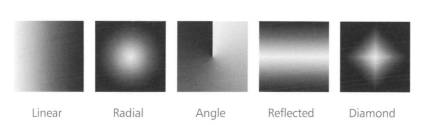

| Linear | Radial | Angle | Reflected | Diamond |

The Paint Bucket Tool

You can use the Paint Bucket tool to color pixels with the foreground color, based on a tolerance setting. It works in a similar way to the Magic Wand tool, but, in this case, filling adjoining pixels that fall within the tolerance setting. You can use the Paint Bucket tool within a selection, or on the entire image.

The Anti-aliased option creates a slightly soft edge in the areas that the Paint Bucket fills.

1 To fill an area with the foreground color, select the Paint Bucket tool. In the Options bar, leave the Fill pop-up set to Foreground. Enter a value from 0-255 in the Tolerance box. The higher you set the value, the greater the range of colors the Paint Bucket fills.

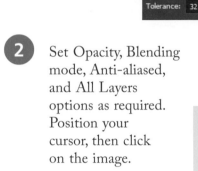

You cannot use the Paint Bucket on images in Bitmap mode.

2 Set Opacity, Blending mode, Anti-aliased, and All Layers options as required. Position your cursor, then click on the image.

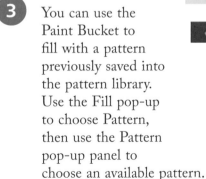

Click the Options menu button (⚙), in the Pattern Fill panel, to access a range of preset pattern fills:

Artist Surfaces
Artists Brushes Canvas
Color Paper
Erodible Textures
Grayscale Paper
Nature Patterns
Patterns 2
Patterns
Rock Patterns
Texture Fill 2
Texture Fill

3 You can use the Paint Bucket to fill with a pattern previously saved into the pattern library. Use the Fill pop-up to choose Pattern, then use the Pattern pop-up panel to choose an available pattern.

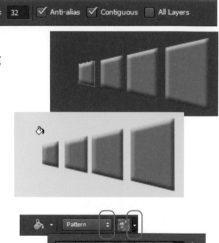

4 Deselect the Contiguous option to allow the Paint Bucket to color pixels anywhere in the image, provided that they fall within the Tolerance setting.

Blending Modes

Choose blending modes from the pop-up menu in the Options bar for each painting tool. The various paint modes, in combination with opacity/pressure settings, have a selective control on which pixels are affected when you use the painting and editing tools. The result is more of a blending of the paint color and the color of the base pixels, than simply one color replacing another.

Dissolve

Produces a grainy, chalk-like effect. Not all pixels are colored as you drag across the image, leaving gaps and holes in the stroke. Reduce the Opacity setting to control the effect.

Clear

Makes pixels transparent. You can only access this mode on a layer with the Lock Transparency option deselected. Available for the Brush, Paint Bucket, Pencil, and Line tools.

Behind

Only available when you are working on a layer with a transparent background. Make sure Lock Transparency is deselected for the layer. Use Behind to paint behind the existing pixels on a layer. Paint appears in the transparent areas, but does not affect the existing pixels.

Darken

Applies the paint color to pixels that are lighter than the paint color – doesn't change pixels darker than the paint color.

Multiply

Combines the color you are painting with the color of the pixels you drag across, to produce a color that is darker than the original colors.

Color Burn

Darkens the base color by increasing the contrast in base color pixels, depending on the blend color. More pronounced when paint color is dark. Blending with white has no effect.

Mode: Normal

Normal
Dissolve
Behind
Clear

Darken
Multiply
Color Burn
Linear Burn
Darker Color

Lighten
Screen
Color Dodge
Linear Dodge (Add)
Lighter Color

Overlay
Soft Light
Hard Light
Vivid Light
Linear Light
Pin Light
Hard Mix

Difference
Exclusion
Subtract
Divide

Hue
Saturation
Color
Luminosity

Don't forget

The blending modes allow you to make changes to an image, using the painting and editing tools in a more selective and subtle way than simply painting with the foreground color. The color you paint with (the blend color) combines with the color of the pixels you drag across (the base color) to produce a different color, depending on the blending mode you select.

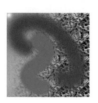

Hot tip

Refer to the original image below for comparison purposes. This image uses Normal blending mode:

Don't forget

Blending modes are also available in the Layers panel, and in the Fill Path, Fill, Stroke, and Fade dialog boxes.

...cont'd

Linear Burn

Darkens the base color by decreasing brightness, depending on the blend color used. Blending with white has no effect.

Lighten

Replaces pixels darker than the paint color, but does not change pixels lighter than the paint color.

Screen

Produces the opposite effect to Multiply. It multiplies the opposite of the original color by the painting color, and has the effect of lightening the pixels.

Color Dodge

Brightens the base color by decreasing contrast. More pronounced when the paint color is light. Blending with black has no effect.

Linear Dodge

Brightens the base color by increasing the brightness, depending on the blend color. Blending with black has no effect.

Overlay

This increases the contrast and saturation, combining the foreground color with the pixels you drag across. Highlights and shadows in the base color are preserved.

Soft Light

Creates a soft lighting effect. Lightens colors if the painting color is lighter than 50% gray, darkens colors if the painting color is darker than 50% gray.

Hard Light

Multiplies (darkens) or screens (lightens) pixels, depending on the paint color, and tends to increase contrast.

Vivid Light

Burns or Dodges base pixel colors, by increasing or decreasing contrast, depending on the blend color.

Linear Light

Burns or Dodges base pixel colors by increasing or decreasing brightness, depending on the blend color.

Pin Light

Replaces base color pixels, depending on whether the blend color is lighter or darker than 50% gray.

Difference

Examines the brightness of pixels and the paint color, then subtracts paint brightness from pixel brightness. Depending on the result, it inverts the pixels.

Exclusion

The result is similar to Difference, but with lower contrast.

Hue

In color images, applies the hue (color) of the paint, without affecting the saturation or luminosity of the base pixels.

Saturation

Changes the saturation of pixels, based on the saturation of the blend color, but does not affect hue or luminosity.

Luminosity

Changes the relative lightness/darkness of the pixels, without affecting their hue or saturation.

Color

Applies the hue and saturation of the blend color; does not affect base pixel luminosity.

Beware

Lighter Color and Darker Color do not create a third "blend" color from the color you paint with and the base color. From a comparison of the total of values in all channels, Lighter displays the lightest color, Darker displays the darkest color:

Creating Rasterized Shapes

A rasterized shape is a shape comprised of pixels. It is not based on a vector path and cannot be edited in the same way as a shape layer.

Beware

You cannot create a rasterized shape on a vector-based shape layer, or a type layer.

1 To create a rasterized shape, select a layer, or create a new layer. Select a foreground color for the shape.

2 Select either the Rectangle, Rounded Rectangle, Ellipse, Line, Polygon, or Custom Shape tool.

3 Select Pixels from the Pick tool mode pop-up in the Options bar.

4 Position your cursor in the image window. Drag diagonally to define the size of the shape. The shape appears in the window. It does not automatically create a new layer. A rasterized shape is the equivalent of creating a selection, then filling it with a color.

Hot tip

To create a custom shape, select the Custom Shape tool, then click on the Shape pop-up triangle in the Options bar to access the default shape library. Click on a shape to select it, then click and drag in the image window to define the size of the shape:

5 For each of the Shape tools you can create custom settings. Click the Geometry Options pop-up triangle to the right of the Custom Shape tool. Each tool has its own specific set of controls.

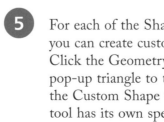

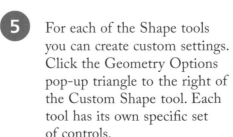

6 The Editing Tools

The editing tools covered in this chapter let you edit or change pixels in a variety of ways. The tools can be used within a selection, or anywhere on an image. Many of the techniques and keyboard shortcuts covered for the painting tools apply to the editing tools as well.

Blur, Sharpen and Smudge

The Blur and Sharpen Tools

The Blur and Sharpen tools are the two "focus" tools. The Blur tool works by reducing contrast between pixels, and can be useful for disguising unwanted, jagged edges and for softening edges between shapes. The Sharpen tool works by increasing the contrast between pixels.

Don't forget

Remember to set an appropriate brush size before you start to work with the Blur/Sharpen tool.

1 To blur or sharpen areas of your image, select the appropriate tool. In the Options bar, set the Blend mode, Strength, and Use All Layers options, position your cursor on the image, then click and drag to blur or sharpen the pixels. Release the mouse, then drag across the pixels again to intensify the effect. You may produce a coarse, grainy effect if you overuse the Sharpen tool. Use a low Strength setting, and build up the effect gradually, each time you drag across the image.

Don't forget

In a document with multiple layers, select the Sample All Layers checkbox in the Options bar, if you want to blur, sharpen or smudge pixels on more than one layer.

The Smudge Tool

Use the Smudge tool to create an effect similar to dragging your finger through wet paint. The Smudge tool picks up color from where you start to drag, and then smears it into adjacent colors.

1 Select the Smudge tool. Set the Strength, position your cursor on the image, then start to drag to smudge the colors. The higher the Strength setting, the more pronounced the effect.

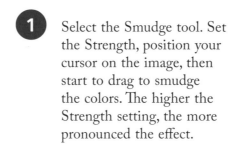

Beware

Each Focus tool retains its own settings when you switch to one of the other tools in the group.

2 Select the Finger Painting option to begin the smudge with the current foreground color. Select the Use All Layers option to smudge colors from other layers in the image onto the layer you are working on. Leave this option deselected if you want the smudge to pick up color from pixels on the active layer only.

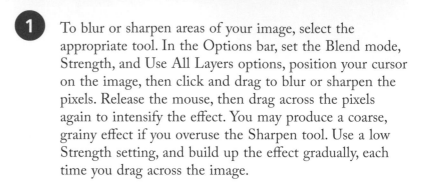

The Clone Stamp Tool

You can use the Clone Stamp tool to retouch an image, by cloning or duplicating areas of pixels. This is very useful when you want to remove blemishes, scratches and other unwanted detail.

1 To clone an area of an image, select the Clone Stamp tool. Set an appropriate brush size, using the Brush Preset Picker in the Options bar. Make sure Aligned is selected.

Use the "[" or "]" keys on the keyboard to decrease/increase the size of editing tool brushes as you work.

2 Hold down Alt/option and click on the part of the image you want to clone – this defines the area of source pixels you use to make the repair.

3 Release Alt/option. Move the cursor to a different image part, then click and drag. The pixels in the image where you drag are replaced by pixels cloned from the spot where you first clicked. A crosshair at the point where you first clicked indicates the pixels that are being cloned – the source point.

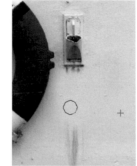

After you Alt/option + click to set the sample point, the Clone Stamp cursor displays a preview of the pixels at the sample point.

87

Clone – Aligned
With Aligned selected, the distance from the source point (shown by the crosshair) to the Clone Stamp cursor remains fixed. When you release the mouse, move the cursor, then continue to use the Clone Stamp tool, the relative position of the source point and the Clone Stamp cursor remains constant, but you will now clone pixels from a different part of the image.

Clone – Non-aligned
With the Aligned option off, the source point – where you first click – remains the same. If you stop dragging with the Clone Stamp cursor, move to a different part of the image then start dragging again, the pixels you clone continue to come from the original source point.

Select which layers you want to include in the clone sample from the Sample pop-up menu. Click the Ignore Adjustment Layers button to exclude Adjustment layers from the sample:

Dodge, Burn and Sponge

The Dodge, Burn, Saturate/Desaturate group of tools are sometimes referred to as the "toning" tools. The Dodge and Burn tools are based on the traditional photographic technique of decreasing the amount of exposure given to a specific area on a print to lighten it (dodging), or increasing the exposure to darken areas (burning-in).

The Dodge and Burn Tools

Use the Dodge tool to lighten pixels in your image; the Burn tool to darken pixels in your image.

Hot tip

It's a good idea to use a low exposure setting when you lighten or darken areas of an image, so you build up the effect gradually.

1 To lighten or darken areas of an image, select the appropriate tool. Remember to choose a suitable brush size. A soft-edged brush usually creates the smoothest result.

Shadows
Midtones
Highlights

2 In the Options bar, set the Range pop-up menu to Midtones, Shadows or Highlights, to limit changes to the middle range of grays, the dark or light areas of the image respectively, and also set Exposure to control the intensity of the tool.

3 Position your cursor on the image, then click and drag to lighten/darken the pixels. Release the mouse, then drag across the pixels again to intensify the effect.

Hot tip

Leave the Protected Tones checkbox selected, to help keep clipping of shadow and highlight detail to a minimum.

The Sponge Tool

You can use the Sponge tool when you want to subtly increase or decrease color saturation in areas of your image.

1 To saturate/desaturate areas of an image, select the Sponge tool. Remember to select an appropriate brush size. Set the Mode pop-up to Saturate or Desaturate. Position your cursor on the image, then click and drag to alter the saturation.

Desaturate
Saturate

Don't forget

Each Toning tool retains its own settings when you switch to another tool in the same group.

The Eraser Tool

Use the Eraser tool to erase portions of your image. The Eraser rubs out to the background color when you are working on the Background layer. It erases to transparency when you are working on any other layer, provided the Transparency Lock option ( ) is not selected in the Layers panel.

Don't forget

Use the Size setting in the Brush Preset Picker panel to specify the Eraser size, when using the tool in Brush and Pencil mode.

1 To erase areas of your image, select the Eraser tool to show Eraser options in the Options bar. Use the bar to specify brush size, Mode, Opacity, Flow, Airbrush build-up, and Erase to History options.

2 Click and drag on your image to erase to the background color, or to transparency, depending on the layer on which you are working.

Opacity
Use the Opacity setting to create the effect of partially erasing pixels in the image.

Mode
Use the Mode pop-up to choose an erase mode. The default is Brush. Block is useful when you need to erase along straight edges. The Block eraser is a fixed-size square.

Erase to History
Use the Erase to History option to return pixels to their status at a particular state in the History panel. Click in the History Brush column, in the History panel, to set the state to which the Erase to History option returns pixels.

Hot tip

Hold down Alt/option with the Eraser tool selected to temporarily access the Erase to History option. Click and drag across modified areas of the image to restore them to the specified state in the History panel.

The Magic Eraser

Use the Magic Eraser tool to erase pixels on a layer to transparency. The Magic Eraser works best when you want to remove the background pixels around a hard-edged object. The Magic Eraser tool erases pixels based on a tolerance level, similar to the way in which the Magic Wand works (see page 103 for information on the Magic Wand).

Hot tip

The Magic Eraser tool is grouped with the Eraser tool. Press and hold on the Eraser tool to access the tools in the tool group. You can also use the keyboard shortcut Shift + E to cycle through the Eraser tools.

1 To use the Magic Eraser tool, first select the layer on which you want to work. Select the Magic Eraser tool to show the Magic Eraser options in the Options bar. Enter a Tolerance value. Set a low Tolerance value to erase pixels that are very similar in color value to the pixel on which you first click. Set a high Tolerance value to select a wider range of pixels.

Hot tip

Select the Sample All Layers option to erase pixels based on a sample that takes into account color values from all visible layers, not only the currently active layer.

2 Set an Opacity value of 100% to erase pixels completely. Set a lower Opacity value to create a partially transparent effect. Select the Anti-aliased option to create a smoother edge when pixels are erased (see page 99 for further information on anti-aliasing).

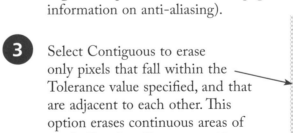

3 Select Contiguous to erase only pixels that fall within the Tolerance value specified, and that are adjacent to each other. This option erases continuous areas of pixels. Deselect Contiguous if you want the Magic Eraser to erase all pixels that fall within the Tolerance value, anywhere in the image.

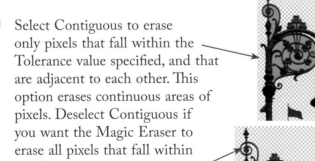

Hot tip

If you use the Magic Eraser on the Background layer, Photoshop automatically converts the layer to Layer 0.

4 Position the cursor, then click to erase pixels that fall within the Tolerance value.

The Background Eraser

Use the Background Eraser tool when you are working on a layer, to erase pixels to transparency. You can set tolerance and sampling values to control the level of transparency and the sharpness of its boundary edges.

1 To erase pixels on a layer, select a layer on which you want to work. Select the Background Eraser tool to show its options in the Options bar. Select a brush from the Brush Presets picker.

Hot tip

Select the Protect Foreground Color checkbox in the Options bar to prevent the tool from erasing pixels that match the current foreground color.

2 Choose Contiguous from the Limits pop-up menu to remove adjacent pixels that fall within the tolerance setting. (Discontiguous erases pixels throughout the image, Find Edges preserves sharp edges along objects.)

Discontiguous
Contiguous
Find Edges

3 Enter a Tolerance value, or drag the Tolerance slider. Set a low Tolerance value to limit the effect to pixels that are very similar in color value to pixels at the "hotspot". Set a high Tolerance value to erase a broader range of similar colors.

Tolerance: 50%

Don't forget

A crosshair at the center of the brush cursor indicates the tool's "hotspot" – the point at which the tool's settings have the greatest effect. The strength of the effect diminishes further away from the hotspot:

4 Choose a Sampling option. Select Continuous to erase all colors that you drag across. Select Once to erase pixels that are the same color as the pixel on which you first click. This is useful when you want to erase areas of solid color. Select Background Swatch to erase areas containing the current background color.

5 Position your cursor, then click or drag to erase pixels on the layer to transparency, based on the settings you have chosen.

The Healing Brush Tool

Use the Healing Brush tools to correct flaws and imperfections in an image. The Healing Brush is similar to the Clone Stamp tool in the way it works, but it also matches the texture, luminosity, and shading of the sampled pixels to the pixels in the area you want to "heal", producing a smooth, seamless result.

Hot tip

Select an option from the Sample pop-up menu to control which pixels are included when you set the sample point by Alt/option clicking:

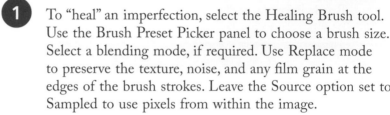

1 To "heal" an imperfection, select the Healing Brush tool. Use the Brush Preset Picker panel to choose a brush size. Select a blending mode, if required. Use Replace mode to preserve the texture, noise, and any film grain at the edges of the brush strokes. Leave the Source option set to Sampled to use pixels from within the image.

2 Select Aligned in the Options bar (see page 87 for information on the Aligned option).

3 Position your cursor on an area of the image you want to sample from, in order to repair the imperfection. Hold down Alt/option, then click the mouse button. This sets the sample area of pixels.

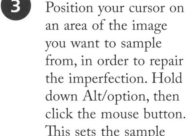

Hot tip

As you work with the editing tools, you can press the square bracket keys – "[" or "]" – to decrease/increase the size of the brush.

4 Release the Alt/option key. Move your cursor over the area you want to repair. Click, or press and drag, to repair the area. When you click or drag the mouse, the (+) indicates the area of the image you are sampling pixels from.

The Spot Healing Brush Tool

Like the Healing Brush tool, the Spot Healing Brush tool removes unwanted detail, and repairs imperfections in an image. The Spot Healing Brush does not require you to set a sample point, it automatically samples pixels in the area of the brush.

Leave the Content-Aware option selected in the Options bar, as this typically produces the best results. Content-Aware makes detailed analysis of neighboring areas to stitch together a realistic and seamless fill.

1 Select the tool, then select a brush size large enough to cover the blemish.

2 Position your cursor on the blemish, then click once to remove it.

3 For larger areas, you can click and drag over the blemish. The Spot Healing brush matches the shading, luminosity, texture, and transparency of pixels, to remove the unwanted detail.

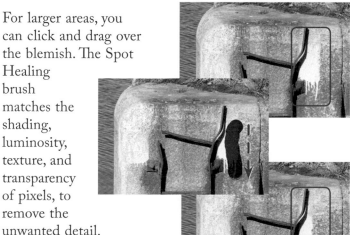

93

For the Spot Healing Brush, the Proximity Match option, available in the Options bar, samples pixels around the tool cursor in order to adjust texture, luminosity, shading, and transparency values, to remove the blemish:

Create Texture analyzes pixels in the area of the brush to create a texture that replaces the blemish:

The Patch Tool

The Patch tool allows you to disguise problems and flaws in an image, by cloning or copying pixels from another, similar part of the image. The Patch tool attempts to match the texture and shading of the pixels that are copied, or sampled, to the source pixels – the pixels you are patching over.

The Content-Aware option, available from the Patch pop-up in the Options bar, allows you to harness the latest content-aware technology using the Patch tool. Content-Aware Patch, unlike the Content-Aware Fill command, allows you to specify the exact area of pixels in the image that is used as the source for the content-aware repair.

See page 96 for information on using settings in the Adaptation pop-up menu.

To fix "red eye" caused by camera flash, select the Red Eye tool, position your cursor on the red eye in the image, then click. In most instances, the default settings work well. Adjust Pupil Size and Darken Pupil settings in the Options bar, if necessary:

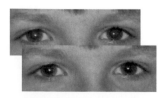

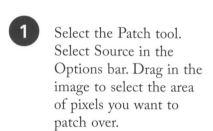

1 Select the Patch tool. Select Source in the Options bar. Drag in the image to select the area of pixels you want to patch over.

2 Still working with the Patch tool, position your cursor inside the Patch selection, then drag the selection area onto the area of the image you want to copy pixels from.

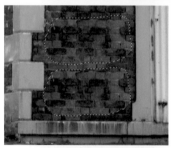

3 Release the mouse button. The original patch selection is repaired with pixels sampled from the area you released on.

4 Alternatively, select Destination in the Options bar to reverse the way in which the tool works. Use the Patch tool to select the area of pixels you want to use to make the repair. Drag the Patch selection onto the area of pixels you want to repair. Release the mouse to copy the initial selection area over the flaw.

Color Replacement Tool

Use the Color Replacement tool to paint over specific colors in an image.

1 To paint over a color, select the Color Replacement tool. Select a foreground color. Create settings, such as Size, using the Brush Preset picker in the Options bar. Leave Mode set to Color.

2 For Sampling, choose Continuous to sample and replace colors continuously as you drag. Choose Once to replace only the target color you first click on. This makes the tool very specific, and typically changes only a limited number of pixels. Choose Background Swatch to limit color changes to pixels that are the same color as the Background color.

3 From the Limits drop down menu, choose Contiguous to color pixels immediately adjacent to the pixels you drag across, and that fall within the Tolerance setting. Choose Discontiguous to color pixels anywhere within the brush diameter, even if the pixels are not immediately adjacent to the pixels you drag across. Choose Find Edges to help preserve sharpness along edge detail as you replace color.

4 Position your cursor on the pixels you want to change. The Color Replacement tool displays a crosshair at the center of the brush cursor. This indicates the tool's "hotspot" – the point at which the tool's settings have the greatest effect. Click and drag to paint over the pixels.

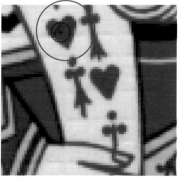

Leave the Anti-aliased option selected, to achieve a smooth edge to the areas where you replace color:

Enter a Tolerance amount, or drag the Tolerance slider to set a Tolerance value. Set a low value to limit changes to pixels that are very similar in color to the pixels at the center of the brush. Set a high value to color a broader range of pixels:

Content-Aware Move Tool

The Content-Aware Move tool provides a quick method for repositioning image content from one area of an image to another. The tool analyzes and blends the pixels you move into their new surrounds and at the same times performs a content-aware fill in the area from which you move the pixels.

Hot tip

In the Adaptation pop-up in the Options bar, enter a value for Structure (1-5) to specify the degree to which Photoshop attempts to retain the background texture as it blends the moved object into its new location. Lower values allow more blending: For Color, enter a value (0-10) to control how much color blending Photoshop applies. Higher values produce greater color blending.

96

Hot tip

To avoid ghosting (see below), to create a more seamless result, expand the selection to include some background pixels surrounding the object you want to reposition. To do this, after you make the initial selection, go to Select > Modify > Expand. Enter a value to expand the initial selection:

1 Start by making a selection around the object that you want to reposition.

2 Select the Content-Aware Move tool from the Spot Healing Brush Tool group. Make sure that the Mode pop-up in the Options bar is set to Move.

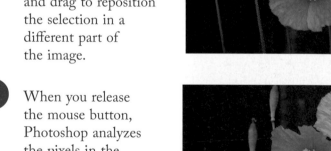

3 Position the Content-Aware Move tool cursor inside the selection, then click and drag to reposition the selection in a different part of the image.

4 When you release the mouse button, Photoshop analyzes the pixels in the selection and the new background context to blend the moved pixels into the new location. At the same

time it performs a content-aware fill on the area from which the pixels were moved. Choose Select > Deselect to accept the move.

7 Selections

One of the most important techniques, when using Photoshop, is making selections. When you make a selection, you are selecting an area of the image you want to make changes to, and isolating the remainder of the image so that it is not affected by changes. A selection is indicated on-screen by a dotted selection marquee.

Marquee Selection Tools

The Marquee selection tools allow you to drag with the mouse to make selections. You can make rectangular or elliptical selections by choosing the appropriate tool.

Beware

If you are working on an image with more than one layer, make sure you select the appropriate target layer before you make a selection.

1 To make a rectangular or oval selection, choose the Rectangular or Elliptical Marquee tool.

2 Position your cursor on the image, then click and drag to define the area you want to select. When you release the cursor, you will see a dotted rectangular or oval marquee defining the area of the selection.

Hot tip

As you are dragging to create a selection, you can hold down the Spacebar to reposition the marquee.

3 Hold down Shift, then click and drag with the Rectangular or Elliptical Marquee tool to create a square or circular selection. Hold down Alt/option, to create a selection from the center out. Hold down Alt + Shift, to create a square or circular selection from the center out.

4 You can reposition the selection marquee, if you need to. Make sure the Marquee tool is still selected, position your cursor inside the selection marquee (the cursor changes shape ▶), then click and drag. You can move selection marquees with any of the Selection tools with the exception of the Quick Selection tool.

Beware

You can only have one selection active at a time, although a selection can consist of several non-contiguous areas.

5 With the Marquee tool selected, you can deselect a selection by clicking inside or outside the selection marquee. Alternatively, you can choose Select > Deselect (Ctrl/Command + D).

Marquee Options

You can use the Marquee Options bar to make changes to the way in which the Marquee tools work.

1 Select the Rectangular or Elliptical Marquee tool. Make sure the New Selection button is selected, in the Options bar.

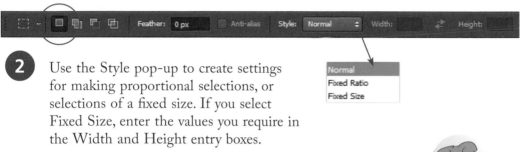

2 Use the Style pop-up to create settings for making proportional selections, or selections of a fixed size. If you select Fixed Size, enter the values you require in the Width and Height entry boxes.

Normal
Fixed Ratio
Fixed Size

3 The Anti-aliased option is an important control when using bitmap applications, such as Photoshop. Select Anti-aliased to create a slightly blurred, soft edge around the selection, and the pixels that surround the selection. Using Anti-aliased helps avoid creating unwanted jagged edges.

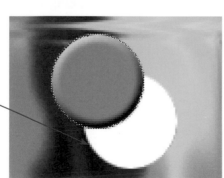

The Anti-aliased option is also available in the Lasso and Magic Wand Options bars.

4 Use the Feather or Refine Edge commands to create a soft, feathered edge (see pages 105-107).

Choose Select > Reselect to reselect your most recent selection. You can use the Reselect command even if you have performed operations and commands on the image since you deselected.

Moving Selected Pixels

You can use the Selection tools to reposition a selection border, but you must use the Move tool if you want to move pixels from one location to another.

Hot tip

With the Marquee, Lasso, or Magic Wand tool selected, position your cursor inside the selection marquee, then hold down Ctrl/Command. The cursor temporarily changes to the Move tool cursor. Click and drag to move the selected pixels.

1 Make a selection. Select the Move tool, then position your cursor inside the Marquee selection border. Click and drag to move the selected pixels.

When you move pixels on the Background layer, the area from where the pixels are moved fills with the current background color. As long as the selection border remains selected, you can continue to move the pixels. Whilst the selection is active, the pixels in the selection "float" above the underlying pixels, without replacing them.

Hot tip

To move the selection in increments of one pixel with the Move tool selected, press the up, down, left, or right arrow keys. Hold down Shift, and press the arrow keys to move the selection in increments of ten pixels.

2 To "defloat" the pixels, so that they replace the underlying pixels, choose Select > Deselect, if you have the Move tool or Magic Wand tool selected. If you used Ctrl/Command with a Marquee or Lasso tool selected, click outside the selection marquee. As soon as you deselect, the pixels on the Background layer underneath the floating selection – the underlying pixels – are completely replaced by the pixels in the floating selection.

3 To move a selection, and make a copy of it at the same time, hold down Alt/option before you drag with the Move tool. The cursor turns into a double-headed arrow (▶), indicating that you are copying the selection.

Don't forget

In a bitmap image, you cannot have an area where there are no pixels. When you move pixels on the Background layer, using the Move tool, the area that was originally selected fills with the current background color.

4 You can turn a "floating" selection into a layer by choosing Layer > New > Layer Via Cut/Layer Via Copy (see Chapter 8, "Layers").

The Lasso Tools

You can use the Lasso tool to make freeform selections by clicking and dragging. It is a useful tool for selecting irregular areas, and for quickly adding to or subtracting from selections made with other selection tools such as the Magic Wand tool.

1 Select the Lasso tool. Set Feather and Anti-aliased options. Position your cursor on the image. The cursor changes to the Lasso cursor. Click and drag around the part of the image you want to select. Make sure your cursor comes back to the start point. If you release before reaching the start point, Photoshop completes the selection with a straight line. A dotted marquee defines the selected area.

Polygon Lasso tool
The Polygon Lasso tool creates a freeform selection with straight line segments.

1 Select the Polygon Lasso tool. Position your cursor on the image, then click; move the cursor, then click… and so on, until you have defined the area you want to select. Click back at the start point to complete the selection. Alternatively, you can double-click to close the selection marquee.

The Magnetic Lasso tool
The Magnetic Lasso tool is most useful when you want to select an object, or an area of the image that contrasts strongly with the area surrounding it.

1 Select the Magnetic Lasso tool. Click on the edge of the object you want to select, to place the first fastening point.

Hold down Shift, then click and drag around an area to add it to the selection. Hold down Alt/option, then click and drag around an area to remove it from the selection.

When you return to the start point with the Polygon Lasso tool, a small circle appears at the bottom right of the cursor to indicate that you can close the selection by clicking once:

You cannot use the Magnetic Lasso tool in 32-bit per channel images.

...cont'd

Hot tip

Click on the edge of the shape, if you need to add a fastening point manually.

Don't forget

The Magnetic Lasso tool adds fastening points at intervals, as you drag the cursor to create the selection. Fastening points anchor the selection border in place as you create the selection, but disappear when you close the selection border.

Hot tip

If the object you want to select has high contrast (i.e. well defined edges), use higher Lasso Width and Edge Contrast settings. For objects with less well defined edges, use lower Lasso Width and Edge Contrast settings.

Either move the cursor along the edge of the object, or click and drag along the edge to draw a freehand segment. As you move along the edge of the object, the "active" segment of the selection border snaps to the most clearly defined edge in the image near the cursor. Fastening points are added automatically, at intervals, as you drag.

2 To close the selection border, position your cursor on the start point, (a small circle at the cursor indicates that you are on the start point) then click. Alternatively, double-click, or press the Enter/Return key. Photoshop creates a segment from the point you have reached to the start point of the selection border. To close the selection border with a straight line segment, hold down Alt/option and double-click.

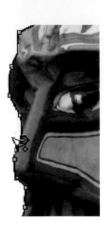

Lasso Width

The Magnetic Lasso tool detects edges within the specified distance from the cursor. Enter a value between 1-256 pixels.

Frequency

This setting determines the rate at which fastening points are set. Enter a value between 0-100. Set higher values to place fastening points at more frequent intervals.

Edge Contrast

Enter a value between 1-100%. This value determines how sensitive the Magnetic Lasso tool is to edges in the image. Higher values select edges that contrast strongly with their background. Lower values select edges that have smaller amounts of contrast.

The Magic Wand Tool

The Magic Wand tool selects continuous areas of color in an image, based on a tolerance setting. Low tolerance settings create a very limited selection of color. Higher settings select a wider range of pixels. The tool is good for selecting areas of reasonably consistent color.

Hot tip

To add to a selection, using the Magic Wand tool, hold down Shift, then click on an unselected part of the image.

1 Before creating a selection using the Magic Wand tool, check the Tolerance setting. Enter a Tolerance value from 0-255. If you set a tolerance value of 255, you will select every pixel in the image.

2 Click on the image, to select pixels of similar color value. All adjacent pixels that are within the Tolerance range are selected. Adjust the default setting of 32 as necessary, to make the selection you require.

Hot tip

Typically, you refine Magic Wand selections by using a combination of the other selection tools, together with the Grow, Similar, and Refine Edge commands.

3 Deselect the Contiguous option to select pixels throughout the image that fall within the Tolerance setting. The result is similar to using the Similar command (see page 109).

4 To deselect a selection marquee when the Magic Wand tool is selected, click inside the selection marquee. If you click outside the selection marquee, you create another selection based around the pixel where you clicked.

Beware

You cannot use the Magic Wand tool in Bitmap mode.

5 If necessary, use the Refine Edge command to evaluate and fine-tune your selection (see page 105 for further information).

The Quick Selection Tool

Using the Quick Selection tool is one of the quickest and easiest ways to select areas of pixels and objects with defined edges.

Hot tip

You can also click with the Quick Selection tool, instead of dragging. This can sometimes make a more precise selection.

1 Click once on the Quick Selection tool to select it. Use the Brush Picker pop-up in the Options bar to set the size of the brush (see page 74 for further information on setting brush options).

2 Click and drag across an area of the image you want to select. The tool samples color in the area, and then forms a selection of pixels which expands outward to defined contrast edges in the image.

Hot tip

Zoom in and work with a smaller brush size to work more precisely when you need to add or remove small areas of pixels in a selection.

104

3 After you create an initial selection with the Quick Selection tool, the Add to Selection option in the Options bar is selected automatically. Click and drag in the image to add further areas to the selection.

4 Select the Subtract from selection tool in the Options bar, then either click or click and drag in the existing selection, to remove areas from the selection.

Sample All Layers – select this option if you want the selection to include pixels from other layers, not just the active layer.

Auto Enhance – select this option to create a more accurate, refined selection. Using this option, Photoshop takes slightly longer to evaluate color values and form the selection.

Hot tip

When using the Add to selection tool, hold down Alt/option to temporarily switch to the Subtract from selection tool.

Refine Edge

After you make a selection with any of the selection tools, you can evaluate and refine the selection edge using the Refine Edge dialog box.

1 To refine a selection, with the selection tool still selected, click the Refine Edge button in the Options bar, or choose Select > Refine Edge.

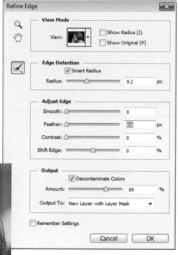

2 Use the View pop-up menu to select a background, against which you can evaluate the results of settings you create in the dialog box. Using different previews helps you to assess the results of settings effectively.

On Black

Overlay

Hot tip

The Zoom and Hand tools are available in the Refine Edge dialog box, so you can move to different parts of the image and zoom in or out, to assess the effect on the selection edge as you make changes to settings.

Hot tip

Select the Show Radius checkbox in the View Mode pane to show the border zone, where Photoshop attempts to refine the selection edge according to the settings you specify. In the screen shot below, the View mode is set to Black:

Hot tip

Whilst using the Refine Edge dialog box, type F on the keyboard to cycle through the previews.

...cont'd

Hot tip

For a selection with a mixture of soft and hard edges, select the Smart Radius checkbox, to create a refinement border that automatically adjusts the border radius, according to the type of edges detected.

Hot tip

Click and hold on the Refine Radius tool to access the Erase Refinements tool.

Use the Erase Refinements tool to remove areas from the refinement border. You can toggle between the two tools as you work by holding down the Alt/ option key.

Hot tip

Select the Decontaminate Colors checkbox, then use the Amount slider if you need to remove distinct color fringes, which can occur around soft-edged selections.

3 Drag the Radius slider, or enter a value in the Radius entry box, to specify the size of the border zone where Photoshop attempts to analyze and refine the selection. Typically, you use larger radius settings for soft-edge selections.

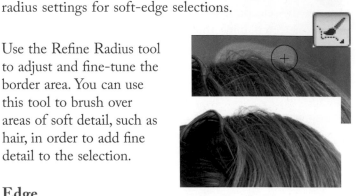

4 Use the Refine Radius tool to adjust and fine-tune the border area. You can use this tool to brush over areas of soft detail, such as hair, in order to add fine detail to the selection.

Adjust Edge

1 Create settings in the Adjust Edge pane, using the Smooth, Feather, Contrast, and Shift Edge sliders to refine the selection.

Smooth – helps smooth jagged edges in a selection, but can sometimes blur fine detail.

Feather – creates a soft-edged selection by blurring it.

Contrast – can remove artifacts (unwanted detail) and make a selection sharper and crisper.

Shift Edges – contracts or expands the overall size of the selection.

Output

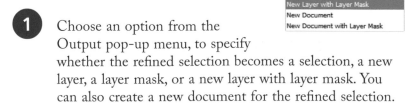

1 Choose an option from the Output pop-up menu, to specify whether the refined selection becomes a selection, a new layer, a layer mask, or a new layer with layer mask. You can also create a new document for the refined selection.

2 Click OK to apply settings to the image.

Feathering Selections

You can use the Feather option to control the degree to which the edge of a selection is softened or faded. Feathering a selection creates a transition boundary between the selection and the surrounding pixels, which can cause a loss of detail.

Beware

Get into the habit of checking for Feather settings in the Options bar before you make a selection, so that you don't create a feathered selection unintentionally.

1 Select one of the Lasso tools, or the Rectangular or Elliptical Marquee selection tool. In the Options bar, set a Feather value, e.g. 10. The amount you set depends on the effect you want to achieve. Use higher values on high resolution images. Create a selection using a selection tool. Alternatively, using any of the selection tools, you can make a selection and then choose Select > Refine Edge. Enter a value in the Feather entry box, or drag the slider.

Feather: 0.0 px

2 When you move the selection, using the Move tool, you will see the feathered edge around the selection, and also where you move the selection from.

Hot tip

You can also feather a selection after you create it by choosing Select > Modify > Feather (Shift+F6).

Creating a vignette

You can use the feathering option to create a vignette, or soft, fading edge to an image.

1 Set a Feather value in the Options bar for the selection tool you are using. Next, create a selection, which can be a regular or irregular shape. Choose Select > Inverse. This reverses the selection – selecting all the pixels that were previously not selected. Press Delete (Mac), or Backspace (Windows). In the Fill dialog box, select Background from the Use pop-up to delete the area surrounding your selection, leaving a feathered edge.

Beware

Feathering, unlike anti-aliasing, blurs the inside and outside of a selection boundary.

Hot tip

Before you make a selection for a vignette effect, make sure you set the background color to white (see page 61).

Modifying Selections

There are many instances when you need to add to or subtract from a selection. You can use any combination of selection tools to make the selection you want. For example, you might start by making a selection with the Magic Wand tool, then add to the selection using the Lasso tool.

Hot tip

To modify an existing selection, select a Selection tool, then click the Add to ... , Subtract from ... , or Intersect with Selection button in the Options bar. These settings remain in effect for the tool:

It's worth reselecting the New Selection button, so previous tool settings do not cause unexpected results the next time you use the tool.

Hot tip

For complex selections, it can be useful to temporarily hide the dotted selection border, in order to see the selected pixels more clearly. Choose View > Show > Selection Edges, to hide the selection border. The selection remains active; you have simply hidden the border. Choose the same option to redisplay the selection border.

1 To add to an existing selection, hold down the Shift key, then click and drag, to create another selection marquee that intersects the existing selection marquee.

2 You can use the same technique to create non-adjoining selections. Although the selections may be in different parts of the image, they count and act as one selection. For example, if you apply a filter, the effect will be apparent in all the selection marquees.

3 To add to a selection, hold down Shift, and use the Lasso tool to quickly loop around small areas that the Magic Wand tool typically misses out from its selection.

4 To subtract from a selection, hold down Alt/option, then click and drag with a selection tool, to intersect the existing selection marquee. The area defined by the intersecting marquee is removed from the original selection.

Grow and Similar Commands

The Grow and Similar commands are very useful when used in conjunction with the Magic Wand tool, to add to a selection. Both work according to the Tolerance value set in the Magic Wand Options bar.

The Grow command selects contiguous or adjoining areas of color, based on the Tolerance setting in the Magic Wand Options bar.

1 Make a selection. Check that the Tolerance setting in the Magic Wand Options bar is appropriate.

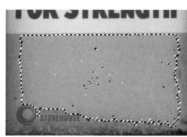

2 Choose Select > Grow to add pixels to the existing selection that fall within the Tolerance setting, and which are adjacent to pixels already in the selection.

If necessary, change the Tolerance setting for the Magic Wand tool before using the Grow command, to achieve a, more or less, inclusive result.

The Similar command selects non-adjacent pixels that fall within the same Tolerance setting, as set in the Magic Wand Options bar.

1 Make a selection using any of the selection tools. Check that the Tolerance setting in the Magic Wand Options bar is appropriate.

2 Choose Select > Similar to select pixels throughout the image that fall within the Tolerance setting.

Using the Magic Wand tool, with Contiguous in the Options bar deselected, is the equivalent of using the Similar command.

Pasting Into Selections

Pasting into selections is useful for compositing images.

Beware

When you paste into a selection, the selection from the Clipboard is rendered at the resolution of the destination document. This means that the selection copied from the source document changes size, if the resolution of the two documents are different.

① Create a selection in the destination window.

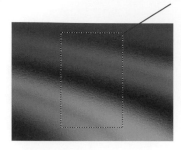 

② Open the source document, then make the selection you want to paste into the destination document. Choose Edit > Copy to copy the selection to the Clipboard.

③ Click in the destination image window. The selection should still be active. Choose Edit > Paste Special > Paste Into, to paste the Clipboard selection into the selected area.

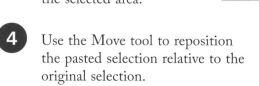

④ Use the Move tool to reposition the pasted selection relative to the original selection.

Hot tip

Make sure the layer mask is selected, then paint with black, to add to the mask, or paint with white to subtract from it (see pages 172-173, "Layer Masks").

⑤ The Paste Into command creates a layer mask. The layer is active, indicated by the highlight border on the thumbnail in the Layers panel, which means that you can edit

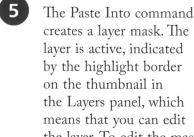 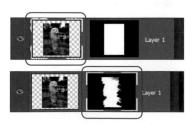

the layer. To edit the mask, click the Mask icon in the Layers panel. The highlight border appears on the mask, to indicate that the layer mask is selected.

Filling a Selection

You can use the Fill dialog box to fill an entire layer or a selection.

1 To fill a selection, first define either a foreground or background color that you want to fill with, then make a selection. Choose Edit > Fill. Select the Use pop-up to choose the fill type. You can also set Opacity for the fill and a Blending Mode. Click OK.

See pages 81-83 for a description of the blending modes.

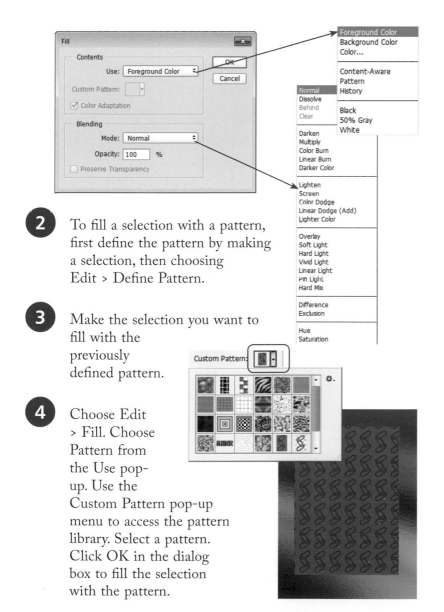

2 To fill a selection with a pattern, first define the pattern by making a selection, then choosing Edit > Define Pattern.

3 Make the selection you want to fill with the previously defined pattern.

4 Choose Edit > Fill. Choose Pattern from the Use pop-up. Use the Custom Pattern pop-up menu to access the pattern library. Select a pattern. Click OK in the dialog box to fill the selection with the pattern.

If you don't make a selection before you choose the Fill command, you fill the entire layer.

...cont'd

Content Aware Fill

The Content-Aware fill option, in the Use pop-up, provides a powerful and time-saving option for adding detail to an image where it doesn't exist, or for seamlessly removing unwanted detail.

Hot tip

Select the Color Adaptation check box to use the most advanced algorithms for blending the fill color into the surrounding area.

1. To add areas to an image, based on detail that currently exists in the image, first make a selection that covers the area of missing detail, and that includes a small overlap into existing detail.

2. Choose Edit > Fill. Select Content-Aware from the Use pop-up menu, then click OK.

3. To remove detail from an image, make a selection around the detail you want to remove, then use the Content-Aware option from the Fill dialog box.

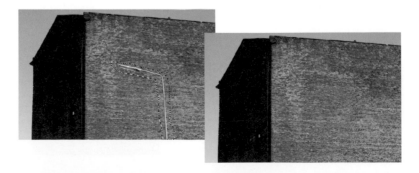

Copying and Pasting Selections

You can use the Clipboard to copy and paste selections within the same image, and into other images. You can also drag selections between images.

1 To copy a selection, first make a selection using any of the selection tools. Choose Edit > Copy.

2 To paste the selection into the same image, choose Edit > Paste. The selection is pasted into the image, on its own layer. (For information on working with layers, see Chapter 8, "Layers".)

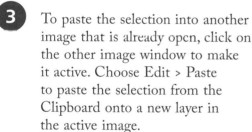

3 To paste the selection into another image that is already open, click on the other image window to make it active. Choose Edit > Paste to paste the selection from the Clipboard onto a new layer in the active image.

4 You can also drag a selection from one floating image window into another. You need two image windows open – the source and the destination windows. Make a selection in the source window, select the Move tool, position your cursor within the selection, then click and drag into the destination window. The selection appears on its own layer.

A useful technique for selecting a simple object, like the flower in this image, is the Inverse selection command. Use the Magic Wand tool to select the background, then choose Select > Inverse to reverse the selection. The areas that represent the flower are now selected.

When you copy and paste content in the same image, the pasted content appears in exactly the same position on the new layer as the original copied selection. In this example, the pasted flower is offset from its original position as pasted, to make the copy obvious in the screenshot.

Working with tabbed image windows, you can drag a selection from one image to another. First make sure you are working with the Move tool. Drag the selection from the source document onto the file name tab of the destination document. When the destination document tab becomes active, drag the cursor down into the image window then release.

Focus Area Selection

The Focus Area selection dialog box allows you to make selections based on areas of an image that are in focus. This is a quick and effective selection technique for isolating in-focus foreground content from its background.

Hot tip

Make a copy of the original Background layer, then use the Focus Area selection dialog box on the copied layer – this allows you to easily step back to the original image or use pixels from the original image to rebuild problem areas.

1 Choose Select > Focus Area. The Focus Area dialog box appears and Photoshop automatically begins to analyze the image for in-focus areas and displays the results on a white matte background.

Hot tip

Use the Preview checkbox to toggle between the original image and the selection to see before and after states.

Hot tip

You can use Ctrl/Command + Z to undo/redo your last step in the Focus Selection dialog box.

2 Use the View mode pop-up menu to view the results on different backgrounds. Viewing using different View mode backgrounds can help you evaluate problem areas where you may need to make further adjustments to achieve a better selection. For example, for this flower image, viewing the Black & White mask reveals areas within the flower that are not selected. (Use the Focus Area Add tool to manually select these areas.)

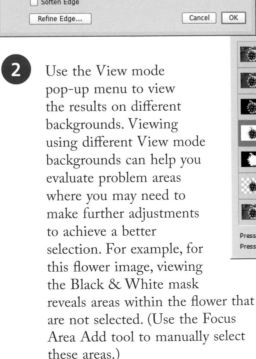

...cont'd

3 Use the Focus Area Add brush ( ) to manually add areas to the initial selection. Use the Focus Area Subtract tool ( ) to remove areas from the selection.

4 In the Parameters pane, the In-Focus Range is set to Auto by default. To set the In-Focus Range manually, drag the slider to the left to include less focused areas of the image; drag to the right to create a more limited selection based on in-focus areas.

5 If necessary, click the Advanced

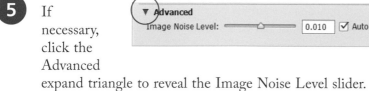

expand triangle to reveal the Image Noise Level slider. In a "noisy" image, if there is too much unwanted noise selected, drag the slider to the right to eliminate the noise artifacts from the selection.

6 Select the Soften Edge checkbox to defringe and slightly feather the selection edge.

7 Click the Refine Edge button to access the Refine Edge dialog box to further fine-tune the initial Focus Area selection. When you OK the Refine Edge dialog box you return to the image window, not the Focus Area dialog box. (See pages 107-108 for information on using the Refine Edge dialog box.)

Hot tip

When using the Focus Area Add/Focus Area Subtract tools, you can type the [or] keys to decrease/increase the size of the brush in increments.

Don't forget

Noise can appear in an image as areas of pixel variation, or color artifacts, which do not represent detail in the image, and are therefore undesirable.

Image noise typically appears either as luminance noise, which tends to make the image appear patchy, or color noise, where irregular color artifacts appear in the image.

Before

After

Transforming Selections

The ability to transform a selection's bounding box enables you to fine-tune selections, distort selections, and make selections that were previously difficult to achieve.

Beware

The Transform Selection bounding box transforms the selection border only. It does not transform the pixels within the selection.

Hot tip

Drag the Reference Point marker ( ) to a new location, to specify the point around which transformations take place.

Hot tip

Press the Enter key on the keyboard, to commit or accept a transformation. Press the Esc key to abandon changes. You can also double-click inside the transform bounding box to accept a transformation.

1 To transform a selection, choose Select > Transform Selection. A bounding box with eight handles appears around the selection. A Reference Point marker appears at the center of the bounding box.

2 To scale a selection, click and drag a handle. The cursor becomes a bi-directional arrow. To scale a selection in proportion, hold down Shift, then drag a corner handle.

3 To rotate a selection, position your cursor just outside the selection border. The cursor changes to a bi-directional, curved arrow. Click and drag in a circular direction.

4 To distort the selection boundary, hold down Ctrl/Command, then drag a corner handle.

5 To create a perspective effect on the selection border, hold down Ctrl/Command + Alt/option + Shift, then drag a corner handle.

6 To shear a selection border, hold down Ctrl/Command, then click and drag a center top/bottom or center left/right handle.

7 Click the Cancel button in the Options bar to reject changes. Click the Commit button to apply the transformation.

8 Layers

Layers introduce considerable flexibility into the way you can work with images. Layers let you keep various image elements separate, so you can make changes to the pixels on one layer without affecting pixels on another.

Additional layers increase the file size of the image. When you finish editing your image, you can flatten the image to merge all layers into a single Background layer.

Working with Layers

When you create or open an image for the first time, it consists of one default layer, called Background. The Background layer is locked by default.

Beware

New layers are created automatically, when you use the Type tool to add text to an image, when you drag or copy a selection into an image from another image, and also when you drag a layer from one document into another.

1 To create a new layer, choose New Layer from the panel menu ( ). Enter a name for the new layer in the Name entry box. You can also choose Opacity and Blending Mode settings at this stage, if required.

2 Alternatively, click once on the New Layer button at the bottom of the Layers panel, to create a new layer with default settings. Hold down Alt/option, then click the New Layer icon to access the New Layer dialog box.

3 Click OK on the dialog box. This creates a new, empty layer, which appears in the Layers panel above the previously active layer. Notice, also, that the file size in the Document Sizes status bar area increases when you paint on, or add pixels to, the layer.

4 To name a layer, position your cursor on the layer's label, then double-click. Enter a new name in the label entry area, then press Enter/Return on the keyboard.

Hot tip

One of the most useful techniques for creating a new layer is to make a selection on a part of the Background layer, then choose Layer > New > Layer via Copy (Ctrl/Command + J). The selection of pixels is copied to a new layer. You can now edit and transform the pixels on the new layer, with the original pixels intact on the Background layer.

5 To delete the active layer, choose Delete Layer from the panel menu. Click Yes or No in the delete warning box. Or drag the Layer name onto the Trash can icon at the bottom of the Layers panel. No warning alert appears if you use this method.

Selecting, hiding and showing layers

You can only paint, edit pixels, or make color adjustments to one layer at a time. This is often referred to as the "target" or active layer.

1 Click on the layer name in the Layers panel to make it active. The layer name highlights, to indicate that it is active. The name of the active layer appears in the title bar of the image window.

`iris_start.psd @ 33.3% (iris, RGB/8*) * ×`

2 To hide the contents of a layer, click the Visibility icon in the leftmost column of the Layers panel. To show a layer, click in the empty box to bring back the Visibility icon ().

Reordering layers

You cannot change the stacking order of the Background layer, but it is often necessary to change the stacking order of other layers, to control which layers appear in front of other layers.

1 To change the layer order, click and drag the layer name you want to reposition. Notice the horizontal bar that appears as you move the layer upwards or downwards. Release the mouse when the horizontal bar appears in the position where you want the layer moved to.

Repositioning layer contents

You can reposition the entire contents of a layer using the Move tool.

1 Click on the layer you want to move in the Layers panel. Select the Move tool, then position your cursor anywhere on the image. Click and drag, to move the layer.

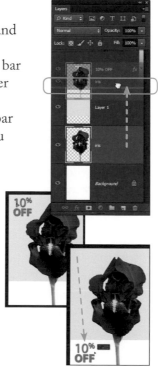

Click the Visibility icon () to hide/show a layer group, and also a layer style.

To select all pixels on a layer, hold down Ctrl/ Command, and click on the layer thumbnail in the Layers panel.

You can nudge the contents of a selected layer in 1 pixel increments by pressing the arrow keys when the Move tool is selected.

Notice the on-screen readout panel that appears as you drag to reposition a layer. The panel displays readouts for vertical and horizontal move amounts and helps you work with accuracy and precision:

Merge and Flatten Layers

Use the Merge commands to combine two or more layers into one layer. This is useful for keeping the file size down, and for consolidating elements on different layers into a single manageable layer or unit.

The Merge Visible Layers command, in the panel menu, merges only the currently visible layers.

When you use the Flatten Image command, if there are hidden layers in the document, a warning prompt appears:

Click OK to flatten the image and delete the hidden layers. Click Cancel to return to the image without flattening it.

When you convert images between some modes, you are prompted to flatten the file. Make sure you save a copy of the file first, if you want to be able to go back and make further changes to the layers.

1 To merge all the visible layers in your document, first hide any layers you don't want to merge. Make sure one of the layers you want to merge is active, then choose Merge Visible from the panel menu ( ) or choose Layer > Merge Visible.

2 To merge a layer with the layer below it, first select the layer, then choose Merge Down, from the panel menu, or choose Layer > Merge Down.

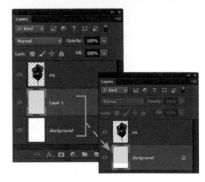

Flattening images

When you flatten an image, you end up with a Background layer only. This reduces the file size. Flatten an image when you have finished creating and positioning the elements of your composite image, and are ready to save the file in a suitable format for placing in a page layout application.

1 To flatten an image, make sure that all the layers you want to keep are visible. Choose Flatten Image, from the Layers panel menu, or choose Layer > Flatten Image.

Moving Layers Between Images

Working in floating windows (Window > Arrange > Float All in Windows), you can copy a complete layer from one Photoshop document to another, similar to the way you move a selection from one document to another.

1 First, make sure you have two document windows open – a "source" document and a "destination" document. The source document contains the layer you want to copy. The destination document is the document into which you want to copy the layer.

2 Click in the source document window, to make it active. Position your cursor on the layer in the Layers panel, then drag the layer you want to copy from the source document into the destination document window. A dimmed layer preview indicates the layer you are copying.

3 Position the layer, and then release the mouse. The layer is positioned above the previously active layer in the destination document's Layers panel. The destination document becomes the active image window.

Beware

The layer you move into the destination image window is rendered at the resolution of that window. This may cause the elements on the moved layer to appear larger or smaller than in the original window. To avoid surprises, make sure that the source and destination images are at the same resolution. Also, if the modes of the two images are different, then the layer you move is converted to match the mode of the destination window.

Don't forget

If necessary, use the Defringe command (Layer > Matting > Defringe) to remove any fringe around pixels on a layer that you copy from one image to another.

Selecting and Linking Layers

Selecting multiple layers creates a temporary grouping that allows you to manipulate two or more layers as a unit. Linking layers keeps the layers grouped, until you unlink them. You can move, align and transform multiple selected layers, or linked layers, and also apply styles from the Styles panel.

Don't forget

Link layers when you want to keep elements of an image on separate layers, but you need to make changes to them as a unit.

1 To select multiple, consecutive layers, select the first layer, hold down Shift, then click the last layer in the range. To select multiple, non-consecutive layers, select the first layer, hold down Ctrl/Command, then click each layer you want to add to the selection.

2 To remove a multiple selection of layers, click on any individual layer in the Layers panel. Or click in an empty area below the bottom-most layer in the panel.

Hot tip

Choose Select > All Layers to select all layers in an image; choose Select > Deselect Layers to have no layer selected.

3 To link layers, select two or more consecutive, or non-consecutive layers. Then click the Link button (🔗) at the bottom of the Layers panel. A link icon appears to the right of a linked layer. When you select a linked layer in the Layers panel, all other layers linked to it display a link icon, to indicate their linked status.

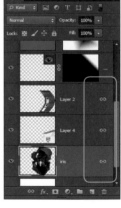

4 To unlink a single layer, select the specific layer you want to unlink, then click the Link button. Other layers in a set of linked layers remain linked.

Don't forget

Use the Move tool to reposition the elements on the linked layers as one.

5 To unlink all layers in a link set, either select each link manually, or select one linked layer, then choose Layer > Select Linked Layers. Click the Link button to unlink all linked layers.

Locking Layers

There are four levels of lock that can be applied to layers. A dimmed lock icon appears to the right of the layer when you select one of the lock options. A solid lock icon appears when the layer is fully locked. There is a move lock on the Background layer by default.

Don't
forget

Transparent areas on a layer are indicated by the checkerboard pattern, when the Background layer is hidden.

1 To completely lock a layer, select the layer in the Layers panel, then click

the Lock All option. You will not be able to reposition the layer, or make any changes to it, including changing blending mode, opacity, and layer style.

2 To prevent the layer from being moved using the Move tool, click the Lock Position option.

3 To disable painting tools on the layer, select the Lock Image pixels option. You can still edit any mask applied to the layer, and you can move the layer. Selecting the Lock Image pixels option automatically locks transparency for the layer.

Hot tip

You can move locked layers to a new position in the stacking order of layers, but you cannot delete a fully locked layer.

4 Click Lock Transparency, to preserve transparent areas of a layer. You can make

changes to the existing pixels on the layer, but you cannot make changes to any areas of transparency. For example, if Lock Transparency is selected, the blur filters do not work effectively on the layer, as pixels cannot spread into the areas of transparency to create the blur effect.

Hot tip

The Lock Transparency and Lock Image Pixels options are automatically selected for Type layers. You cannot turn these options off.

Layer Groups

When you create complex images with multiple layers, it is convenient to simplify the Layers panel by combining related layers together into a layer group. Creating layer groups in complex, multi-layered images makes it much easier to manage the elements in the image.

Hot tip

In the New Group from Layers dialog box, leave the Mode option set to Pass Through, to ensure that blending and opacity settings apply to all layers in an image, and are not limited to the layers in the layer set.

1 To create a new layer group, click the Create New Group button ( ), in the bottom of the Layers panel, to use the current default settings, or choose New Group from the panel menu.

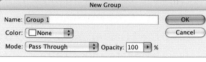

2 To create a layer group from existing layers, first select the layers you want to combine into a layer group. Choose New Group From Layers, in the panel menu ( ), or choose Layer > New > Group from Layers.

Hot tip

To nest a layer group within another layer group, drag the layer group you want to nest onto an existing layer group folder.

3 To move a layer into a layer group, drag it onto the layer group folder. Release the mouse when the layer group folder highlights. The layer is positioned at the bottom of the layers already in the layer group. If the layer group is expanded, drag the layer to the desired position. Release when the highlight bar is in the correct position.

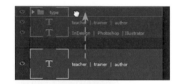

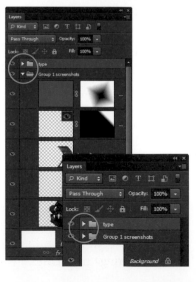

Hot tip

To delete the group folder, but not the layers inside it, choose Delete Group, from the panel menu. In the confirmation dialog box, select Group Only.

4 Click the Collapse/ Expand triangle to reveal or hide the layers contained within the layer group.

Layer Styles

Use the Layer Style sub-menu to create sophisticated layer effects, such as soft shadows, beveled and embossed edges, and inner and outer glows, quickly and easily. The following example consists of three layers – a white Background layer, a colored circle Shape layer, and a colored triangle Shape layer, and uses Bevel and Emboss options to demonstrate the principles for creating a layer style.

1 To apply a layer style, click on a layer in the Layers panel to make it active. Choose Layer > Layer Style > Bevel & Emboss. In the Structure section, choose a style from the Style pop-up menu, and a technique from the Technique pop-up menu. Select the Up/Down radio button to light the effect from above or below.

2 Use the Depth entry box, or slider, to adjust the height of the effect. Use the Size slider to control the spread of the bevel. The Soften slider controls the overall intensity of the effect, and helps reduce irregularities or artifacts in the effect, creating a smoother result.

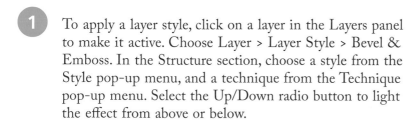

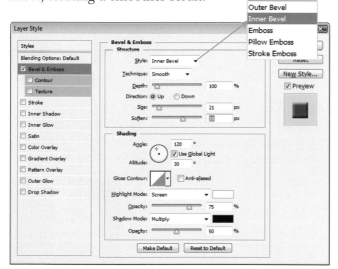

3 In the Shading area, enter a value in the Angle entry box to control the direction of the light source. Enter a value in the Altitude entry box to define the apparent depth of the light source. Drag in the Angle/Altitude disk to create settings manually, if you prefer.

You can also select a layer style option, using the Add Layer Style button at the bottom of the Layers panel:

Each layer style provides a range of options specific to that style. Experiment with the options to achieve the effect you want.

In the Layer Style dialog box, make sure the Preview option is selected, to see the effect applied in the image as you create and edit settings:

...cont'd

You cannot apply a layer style to the Background layer or a locked layer.

4 Gloss Contour allows you to change the transition of the effect across the affected pixels on the layer.

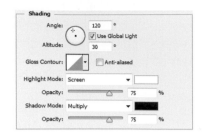

5 Adjust settings for the Highlight and Shadow edges of the effect. It is a good idea to initially leave the blending modes set to Screen and Multiply, respectively. Experiment with the Opacity sliders to create a more subtle effect.

Click on the Expand/ Collapse triangle to hide or show the layer styles applied to a layer:

6 Click OK in the dialog when you are satisfied with the results. In the Layers panel, notice a *fx* symbol on the layer, indicating that there is a layer effect applied to the layer. Whilst the *fx* symbol appears, the layer effect remains editable.

Managing Layer Styles

Once you have created a layer style, you can continue to edit the effect, and you can use a variety of commands from the Layer Style sub-menu to manage the effects.

Click the Visibility icon, to the left of the layer effect, to control its visibility:

1 To edit layer style settings, select the layer, then click the Expand triangle to display layer effects, as separate entries in the Layers panel. Double-click the name of the effect you want to edit. You can adjust settings as often as you need, to achieve the desired result.

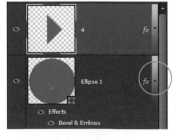

2 To keep the angle of the light source constant, if you are using layer effects on more than one layer in an image, choose Layer > Layer Style > Global Light. Enter a value for the Angle, in the Angle entry box. Click OK on the dialog box. Make sure you select the Use Global Light checkbox in the Layer Style dialog box, when you create multiple layer effects.

3 To copy exact layer style settings from one layer to another, first select a layer with a layer effect applied to it, then choose Copy Layer Style, from the Layer Style sub-menu. Click on another layer in the Layers panel. Choose Paste Layer Style, from the Layer Style sub-menu.

4 To permanently remove layer styles from a layer, make sure you select the appropriate layer, then choose Layer > Layer Style > Clear Layer Styles.

5 Layer styles automate procedures that, in the past, you had to perform yourself. Use the Create Layer command, from the Layer Styles sub-menu, to separate the layer effect into the multiple layers that Photoshop uses to create the effect. This can be useful if you need to manually edit specific parts of the effect.

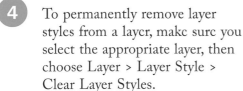

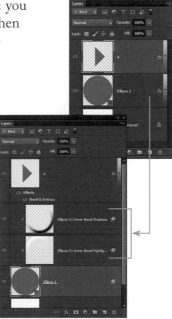

To temporarily disable layer effects on all layers, not just the active layer, choose Layer > Layer Style > Hide All Effects. Choose Layer > Layer Style > Show All Effects, to reverse the process.

You can also drag layer effects from one layer to another to copy the effect. First, make sure you can see the effect entry you want to copy, position your cursor on the entry, hold down Alt/option, then drag the effect to the layer where you want to copy the settings.

Once you merge a layer with a layer effect applied to it, you can no longer adjust the layer effect settings.

Transforming Layers

Beware

To use Perspective and Distort transformations on a Type layer, you must first render (convert to pixels) the Type layer – Layer > Rasterize > Type.

Hot tip

Position your cursor inside the bounding box, then click and drag, to reposition the layer whilst the transformation bounding box is still active.

Hot tip

The Transform sub-menu (Edit > Transform) provides further options for transforming layers.

Once you have moved pixels to a new layer, you can then transform the layer. Using Free Transform, you can scale, rotate, distort, skew, and create perspective effects.

1 Ensure the layer is active. Choose Edit > Free Transform. A bounding box with handles appears around the pixels. To scale a layer, drag a handle. To scale in proportion, hold down Shift, then drag a corner handle.

2 To rotate a layer, position your cursor slightly outside of the bounding box. The cursor changes to a bi-directional arrow. Drag in a circular direction. You can drag the Reference Point marker to a new position, to specify the point around which the rotation takes place.

3 To skew the layer, hold down Ctrl/Command + Shift, then drag the center top/bottom, or the center left/right handle.

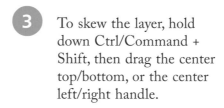

4 To create perspective, hold down Ctrl/Command + Alt/option + Shift, then drag a corner handle. To distort the layer, hold down Ctrl/Command, then drag a corner handle. This allows you to move corner handles independently.

5 Click the Cancel button in the Options bar, or press Esc, to revert to the original state without making changes. Click the Commit button, or press Return/Enter, to accept the transformation and remove the Transformation bounding box.

New Layer Commands

The New Layer via Cut (Ctrl/Command + Shift + J) and the New Layer via Copy (Ctrl/Command + J) commands are essential options when creating layers. Use these commands to either cut or copy selected pixels to a new layer.

129

1 Start by making a selection. Then choose Layer > New > Layer via Copy, to create a new layer containing a copy of the selected pixels. The new layer is automatically named Layer 1, 2, etc., depending on the number of layers already in the document. The new layer is created above the layer that is active when you choose the Layer via Copy command.

2 Make a selection, then choose New Layer via Cut, to cut the selected pixels to a new layer. Notice that when you reposition the pixels on the new layer, the area on the Background layer, from which they were cut, is filled with the current background color.

As you add more and more layers of different types to a document, managing and identifying them becomes more of a challenge. You can use the Filter buttons at the top of the Layers panel to quickly find particular layers you want to work with.

Click the On/Off button (▪) to turn layer filtering on or off. Click one of the filter buttons to limit the layers displayed to specific layer types. In this example, only Type layers are visible in the Layers panel:

You can also use the Filter pop-up to create searches to filter on more specific layer criteria such as Name, Effect and Mode:

Smart Objects

Smart Object layers provide enhanced flexibility as you work in Photoshop, as they can be edited outside the parent file, as independent components. Also, you can make repeated edits and transformations to Smart Objects, without degrading image quality. You can import vector Smart Objects from Adobe Illustrator, or you can create Smart Objects from selected layers within Photoshop.

Vector Smart Objects from Illustrator

Pasting or placing Illustrator artwork as a vector Smart Object allows you to make multiple, non-destructive changes to the artwork in Photoshop. Photoshop achieves this by retaining a link to the original Illustrator artwork, which it then continues to reference as you edit and transform it.

Hot tip

Working with Smart Objects, externally to the parent document, can make it easier to edit specific elements within a complex Photoshop project.

Don't forget

Think of Smart Objects as child elements, or embedded files, that exist within the main parent Photoshop document.

Hot tip

Double-clicking a Vector Smart Object layer launches Illustrator, if it is not already running.

1 Working in Illustrator, select the artwork you want to use as a Smart Object in Photoshop. Choose Edit > Copy to copy the artwork to the clipboard.

2 In a Photoshop file, choose Edit > Paste. In the Paste dialog box, select the Smart Object radio button. Click OK.

3 The Illustrator artwork appears in a bounding box in the center of the screen area. Position your cursor inside the bounding box, then click and drag to reposition the object, if necessary. Drag bounding box handles to scale the artwork to the required size. Hold down Shift, then drag a corner handle to scale the object in proportion.

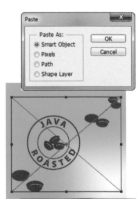

4 Click the Commit button in the options bar when you are ready to place the object on a new layer, as a Smart Object. Or press enter on the keyboard. The object

creates a Vector Smart Object layer. The Smart Object icon appears in the layer thumbnail in the Layers panel, to indicate that it is a Smart Object layer.

Beware

You must keep the Illustrator file in the same folder location, and with the same name, for Photoshop to work with it as a Smart Object.

5 To edit the original Smart Object element in Illustrator, either double-click the Vector Smart Object thumbnail, or make sure the layer is active, then choose Edit Contents from the Layers panel menu. A warning dialog box reminds you to save any changes you make in Illustrator, so that the Photoshop document updates accordingly when you return to it.

Smart Objects from Photoshop Layers

1 To create a Smart Object from existing Photoshop layers, first select one or more layers. Choose Convert to Smart Object, from the Layers panel menu. The selected layers convert to a single Smart Object layer.

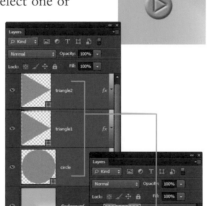

Beware

You cannot apply Perspective, Distort, or Warp transformations to Smart Objects.

131

2 To edit the Smart Object layer as an independent file, double-click the Smart Object layer thumbnail. A warning message reminds you to choose File > Save, to commit any changes you make to the external Smart Object.

Beware

You can also create Smart Object layers using the Place Embedded command. (See pages 34-35.)

3 To return to the parent Photoshop document, and update it with changes made to the Smart Object externally, close the Smart Object window. Click save, if prompted.

Hot tip

Choose File > Open As Smart Object, to open a vector or bitmap file as a Smart Object.

Linked Smart Objects

The Place Linked command allows you to bring content into your Photoshop file by creating a link to an external Photoshop or Illustrator document, instead of embedding the contents within your Photoshop file.

Beware

Because a Linked Smart Object is an external file, you cannot make changes to its pixel data – for example, changing the color, dodging, sharpening or cloning within the Photoshop document.

1 Choose File > Place Linked. Navigate to the location of the file on your system. Click once on the file to select it, then click the Place button.

2 Click OK in the Open As Smart Object dialog box. The external file appears in the image in a bounding box. Use the resize handles to change the size of the placed content and drag the bounding box to a new position if desired. Click the Commit button in the Options bar, press Return/Enter, or double-click inside the bounding box to place the content.

3 The linked smart object appears on a new layer in the Layers panel. A chain icon in the

bottom right corner of the thumbnail indicates that this is a linked smart object layer – the content of the file is not embedded in your Photoshop document.

Don't forget

Transformations such as scaling, skewing, applying perspective and warping affect the version of the linked object within your Photoshop document – they do not change the original, external linked object itself.

4 If the original source file is edited when the Photoshop file that links to it is open, the layer updates immediately. If the original source file is edited when the Photoshop file is closed, when you next open the Photoshop file, a warning icon appears in the Linked Smart Object layer to indicate that the source document has changed. Make sure the layer is selected, then choose Layer > Smart Objects > Update Modified Content.

Warping

Warping is a type of transformation that allows you to bend objects on layers, to create interesting effects, or to map objects to curved surfaces. You can create custom warp effects manually, or you can choose from a variety of warp styles, which you can then customize to meet your requirements.

You cannot apply Warp transformations to Vector Smart Object layers.

1 To warp a selected layer, choose Edit > Transform > Warp. A default warp mesh appears on the contents of the layer.

2 To manually create a custom warp effect, you can drag any of the warp gridlines, drag within any of the mesh segments, or you can drag any of the corner anchor points, or direction points that appear around the edge of the warp mesh. These direction points function in the same way as direction points on a curve segment of a path (see Chapter 10, "Paths" for further details).

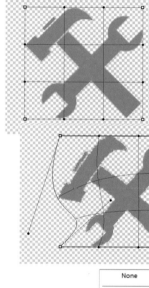

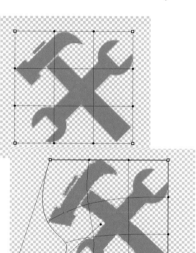

You can use Edit > Undo to undo the last custom warp adjustment.

Using Warp Presets

1 To warp a selected layer using a preset style, choose Edit > Transform > Warp.

2 Select a warp preset from the Warp style pop-up menu in the Options bar.

133

...cont'd

3 To customize the preset warp style, either drag the Bend anchor point, which appears on the warp mesh, or enter a value in the Bend entry box in the Options bar.

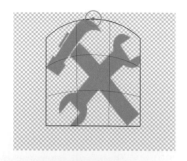

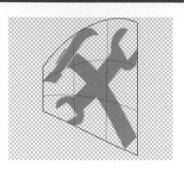

4 In the Options bar, you can enter values in the H entry box (-100–100) to apply horizontal distortion. Enter a value in the V entry box (-100–100) to apply vertical distortion.

5 Click the Change Warp Orientation button in the Options bar, to apply the warp from the opposite orientation.

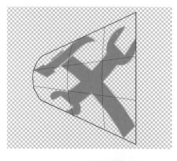

6 Click the Cancel button in the Options bar, or press Esc to revert to the original state without making changes. Click the Commit button, or press Return/Enter to accept the warp transformation and remove the warp mesh.

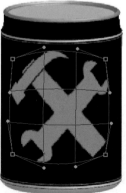

Hot tip

Click the Switch Warp button in the Options bar to switch from a warp mesh to a standard free transform bounding box, or vice versa:

Auto-Align/Blend Layers

Auto-Align Layers and Auto-Blend layers work with content arranged on different layers in an image. To use the Auto-Align/Blend commands, select two or more layers in the layers panel.

Auto-Align Layers

Auto-Align aligns layers based on similarities in image content. It can be used to create panoramic effects, or to align layers with similar content, so you can create a composite image by painting in preferred content from another aligned layer.

1 To align two or more selected layers, choose Edit > Auto-Align Layers. Select a Projection option, in the Auto-Align Layers dialog box.

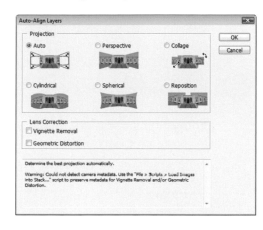

2 To create a composite image from aligned layers, create a layer mask on the topmost layer (see pages 172-173 for information on layer masks). With the layer mask selected, select the Paintbrush tool. Select a soft edge brush, then paint with black to hide pixels on the mask, and allow pixels on the layer below to show through.

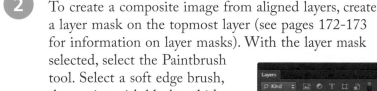

Based on an analysis of the layers, Auto uses Perspective or Cylindrical to produce the best result. Start with Auto, which generally gives good results, but be prepared to experiment with the other projection settings, depending on your original images.

135

Select the Vignette Removal checkbox, to reduce darkening that may occur in the corners and along edges of an image. The Geometric Distortion option can help reduce barrel, pincushion, or fisheye distortion.

...cont'd

Beware

You can only use Auto-Blend Layers for RGB or Grayscale images.

Auto-Blend Layers

Auto-Blend works by applying layer masks to layers, and is useful for stitching together a panorama, or for situations where you have several images of the same composition, but with different areas of in-focus content in each, and you want to create a final image that is a composite of the correctly focused content.

1 Use the Auto-Align Layers command to create a panorama, or a stack of image content, by matching overlapping content for two or more selected layers. When you are satisfied with the alignment, choose Edit > Auto-Blend Layers.

Hot tip

Select the Seamless Tones checkbox to allow Photoshop to blend variations in color and tone, to reduce obvious seams in the final image.

2 For a panorama, select the Panorama blend method. Photoshop creates layer masks for each layer as required, to mask out areas where exposure may vary, resulting in smooth transitions between image detail on individual layers.

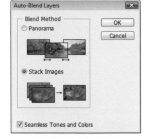

3 Select Stack Images, if you want Photoshop to analyze variations of the same image composition and combine the in-focus parts of each to create the final composite image, which has an increased depth of field. Again, Photoshop uses layer masks to achieve the result.

Beware

Make sure you select two or more unlocked layers before using the Auto-Align Layers command.

The Styles Panel

When you want to apply layer style effects consistently and quickly, it is easy to save layer styles in the Styles panel for later use. Photoshop ships with a wide variety of preset styles, which you can use as the basis for experimentation.

Styles apply to layers – you cannot apply a style to the default Background layer.

Creating Styles

1 Click the Styles panel icon, if the panel is in the Panel dock, or choose Window > Styles to show the panel.

2 Create a layer style, using the custom layer effects you want to include when you save the style (see pages 125-127 for information on working with layer styles). Make sure the layer remains active.

3 Choose New Style from the Styles panel menu ( ). Enter a name for the style in the New Style dialog box, then click OK. The new style appears in the Styles panel.

Applying Styles

1 In the Layers panel, select a layer you want to apply a style to.

2 Click on a style in the Styles panel to apply it to the selected layer. To remove a style from a layer, click the No Style button ( ) in the Styles panel.

Hot tip

You can apply styles to Type and Shape layers, without having to rasterize them first.

...cont'd

3 In the Layers panel, the 🅵 icon indicates a style applied to the layer. Click the expand triangle to show/hide the layer style effects applied to that layer.

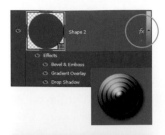

4 Click the Visibility button (👁) to hide or show individual layer effects, or all layer effects.

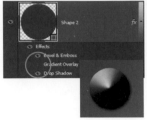

Editing Styles

1 To edit an individual layer effect, double-click the layer effect name in the Layers panel. This takes you back into the Layer Style dialog

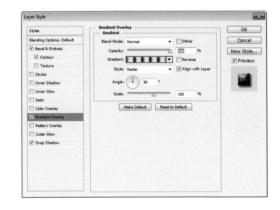

box, which displays the settings currently in force. Adjust settings to create the effect you require. Make sure the Preview checkbox is selected, to see the results of changes you make to settings reflected in the image.

Appending Styles

1 Use the Styles panel menu (▤) to load collections of preset styles that are shipped with Photoshop. Click the Append button to retain the default styles, and add the selected collection to the panel.

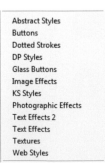

Abstract Styles
Buttons
Dotted Strokes
DP Styles
Glass Buttons
Image Effects
KS Styles
Photographic Effects
Text Effects 2
Text Effects
Textures
Web Styles

Hot tip

Applying a preset style from the Styles panel, then examining and editing the settings used to create the overall effect, is a really good way to build your understanding of the capabilities and potential offered by layer styles.

Hot tip

Choose Reset Styles from the Styles panel menu to return to the original default styles.

138

Content Aware Scaling

The Content Aware Scale command is an automated and intelligent scaling method that analyzes the content of an image, so when you scale the image, key areas of visual importance are preserved during the scaling operation. It is possible, using this technique, to scale a landscape image to portrait proportions, and vice versa.

You can use content-aware scaling on selections and layers, but not the Background layer.

1 To scale a layer, first make sure it is not a Background layer.

If necessary, you can double-click a Background layer in the Layers panel, then click OK in the New Layer dialog box, to convert it to a non-background layer (Layer 0).

2 Choose Edit > Content Aware Scale. A bounding box with eight handles appears around the contents of the layer. A Reference Point marker appears at the center of the bounding box. This is the default point, around which scaling takes place.

Content-aware scaling attempts to limit scaling in images to areas that do not hold distinctive visual detail.

3 Drag a resize handle to scale the image overall, whilst preserving significant visual detail. Hold down Shift, then drag a corner handle to scale in proportion.

4 After you choose the Content Aware Scale command, you can also use options in the Options bar to control the content-aware scaling. You can use the Reference Point Location control to specify the point around which the scaling transformation takes place, then use the X/Y-axis boxes to scale the image to a specific size, or the W/H Scale Percentage boxes to scale the image as a percentage

Click the Protect Skin Tones button ( ), in the Options bar, to help avoid unwanted scaling in people.

139

...cont'd

of its current size. Use the Amount entry box to specify the ratio of content-aware scaling to normal scaling.

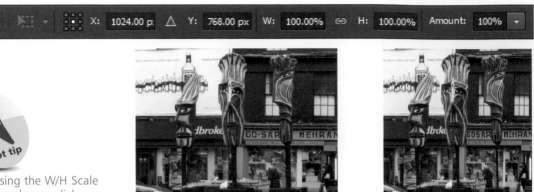

Hot tip

When using the W/H Scale Percentage boxes, click the Maintain Aspect Ratio button (⊖) to scale in proportion.

Before   After

Protecting areas from scaling

You can use an alpha channel to identify an area of an image that you want to protect from scaling.

1 To further protect areas of an image as you use the Content Aware Scaling method, first make a selection, and then save this as an alpha channel (see pages 170-171 for further information).

Beware

You cannot use content-aware scaling on adjustment layers, layer masks, channels, Smart Objects, multiple selected layers or layer groups.

2 Then, before you begin to drag a resize handle to scale the layer contents, select the alpha channel

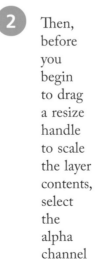

from the Protect pop-up menu.

Puppet Warp

Puppet Warp applies a warp mesh to the contents of a layer. You can add pins to the warp mesh, to create hinge points around which you can bend and transform parts of the image.

To distort a layer non-destructively, using Puppet Warp, first convert the layer to a Smart Objects layer (see page 130). Then, if you decide later that you don't want the warp distortion, you can simply discard the Puppet Warp effect from the Smart Objects layer.

1 To take a layer into Puppet Warp mode, select the layer in the Layers panel.

2 Choose Edit > Puppet Warp. A warp mesh appears on the content of the layer. To control the accuracy of the warp, by creating a finer or coarser mesh, select an option from the Density pop-up menu in the Options bar.

3 Use the Mode pop-up menu, in the Options bar, to control the degree of the warp effect. Distort mode creates the most extreme and dramatic results.

4 Enter a value in the Expansion entry box, or drag the Expansion slider to expand or contract the warp mesh around the contents of the layer.

5 Click on the warp mesh to set a pin. Set two or more pins. Click on a pin to make it active – the active pin has a black circle at its centre.

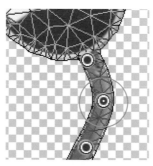

6 Drag the active pin to create the distortion. The non-active pins act as hinge points, anchoring parts of the image in place.

Click the Show Mesh checkbox to hide or show the puppet warp mesh, as required. Hiding the mesh does not hide warp pins:

...cont'd

7 To exit Puppet Warp mode and apply changes, click the Commit button in the Options bar, or press the Enter/Return key. To cancel changes, click the Cancel button, or press the Esc key.

Working with pins

1 To select multiple pin points, click on a pin to select it, then hold down Shift, and click on additional pins to add them to the selection. If you drag any of the selected pin points, you manipulate all selected points at the same time.

2 Select a pin point, then use the Up, Down, Left or Right arrow keys to nudge the pin in 1 pixel increments. Hold down Shift, then use the arrow keys to move the selected pin in 10-pixel increments.

3 Select a pin, then hold down Alt/option (but make sure your cursor is not positioned directly on top of the pin) to access the pin rotate control. Click and drag the cursor in a circular direction to rotate the mesh around the pin. You can also enter a value in the Rotate field in the Options bar, to rotate the selected pin a fixed amount.

4 To delete a pin, select it, then press the Backspace or Delete key. Alternatively, position your cursor on a pin, hold down Alt/option, then click when you see the scissors cursor.

5 To remove all pins, and return the mesh to its original state, click the Remove All Pins button in the Options bar.

Hot tip

If you create a warp effect where one area of an image overlaps another, you can control which area appears in front, using the Pin Depth buttons to move a selected pin forward or backward:

Perspective Warp

The perspective warp mode allows you to make adjustments to perspective in an image and can be useful for adjusting perspective on architectural subjects. You start by establishing the perspective grid and then adjusting points and planes on the grid.

Forming the grid

1 Choose Edit > Perspective Warp. The Perspective Warp tools appear in the Options bar and the Perspective Warp cursor appears in the image window.

2 Locate appropriate suitable verticals or horizontals in the image (such as the corner of the building in this screen shot), then click and drag in the image to create the first warp grid or "quad".

3 Drag the quad points (⚫) to align the perspective grid to match perspective in the image. In architectural images, using architectural detail such as roof lines, ledges, columns and vertical detail in the image can help to create accurate perspective.

4 To create a second perspective quad to define an additional perspective plane, using the Perspective Warp cursor drag inward toward the vertical of the first perspective quad. As the cursor approaches the initial vertical, both highlight in blue lines (see screen shot) to indicate a lock.

Hot tip

It's a good idea to make a copy of a layer (see page 129), before you apply perspective warp adjustments so that you can easily revert to the original if required.

Hot tip

When defining the initial perspective quads, hold down Shift, then drag one of the vertical or horizontal edges to extend the perspective grid, maintaining the current grid perspective.

...cont'd

Hot tip

Click the Layout button in the Perspective Warp options bar if you need to return to the initial perspective quads to re-adjust them.

5 Drag the perspective points on the second quad as you did for the first.

Manipulating the grid

Once you form an accurate and usable perspective grid, you can then start to manipulate the grid to make adjustments as required.

1 Click the Warp button in the Options bar to activate Warp mode. The inner gridlines of the grid disappear and each corner pin highlights.

2 Drag individual pins to warp perspective in the image. You can also click the arrow keys to nudge a selected pin in increments.

3 Hold down Shift, then click an edge to lock it to vertical or horizontal – the line turns yellow. If you drag a pin at either end the edge remains vertical/horizontal.

Before Automatically Straighten near vertical lines

4 Click the Automatically straighten near vertical lines or the Automatically level near horizontal lines to allow Photoshop to analyze the image and perform an automatic adjustment. Click the Remove Warp button to return to the point at which you clicked the Warp button.

After

5 Use the Cancel/Commit button to either reject or accept the perspective warp transformations when you are ready.

9 Working with Type

Type is not always an essential ingredient of an image, but when you need it, Photoshop offers a full range of powerful, sophisticated typesetting controls.

Creating Point Type

You can create two kinds of type: point type and paragraph type. Typically, you use point type when you want to work with small amounts of text, such as a single character, word, or line. Use paragraph type when you are working with more extensive blocks of type in paragraphs.

You can also commit type by pressing the Enter key on the numeric keypad, or selecting any other tool in the Tool panel.

You must be in text editing mode to enter, edit, or format text.

Typekit, available in Photoshop CC 2014, delivers and syncs fonts from an external Typekit server that you connect to via Creative Cloud. Typekit fonts are not installed locally on your computer. To add a font from Typekit choose Type > Add fonts from Typekit. The Typekit icon (𝓉𝓀) appears in the Font list to indicate a Typekit font.

1 To create point type, select the Horizontal Type tool. You can create settings for the type using options in the Options bar, or the Character and Paragraph panels, before you enter the type, or you can format the type after you enter it.

2 Position your cursor in the image window, then click to place the text insertion point. Clicking with the Horizontal Type tool takes Photoshop into text editing mode.

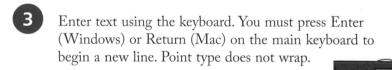

3 Enter text using the keyboard. You must press Enter (Windows) or Return (Mac) on the main keyboard to begin a new line. Point type does not wrap.

4 Click on the Commit button in the Options bar when you have finished entering or editing type, to commit the Type layer. This takes Photoshop out of text editing mode, and you can now perform other tasks on the image. The type appears on its own layer. Or, click the Cancel button to discard the type.

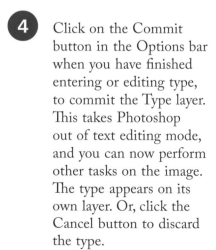

Creating Paragraph Type

When you work with Paragraph type, you define the width of the column of text. The text wraps to a new line when it reaches the edge of the type bounding box.

1 To create Paragraph type, select the Horizontal Type tool. You can create settings for the type, using options in the Options bar, or the Character and Paragraph panels, before you enter the type, or you can format the type after you enter it.

2 Position your cursor at one corner of the type area you want to create. Drag diagonally to define the size of the type's bounding box.

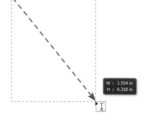

3 Alternatively, with the Horizontal Type tool selected, you can hold down Alt/option, then click in the image to access the

Paragraph Text Size dialog box. Enter values for Width and Height, then click OK.

4 Enter text using the keyboard. Text wraps when it reaches the edge of the type bounding box. Press Enter/Return on the main keyboard only when you want to begin a new paragraph.

5 Click on the Commit button in the Options bar to accept the Type layer. Or click the Cancel button to abandon changes. Both buttons take Photoshop out of text editing mode, and you can now perform other tasks on the image. The type appears on its own layer.

Hot tip

If you enter more type than can fit in the type bounding box, an overflow symbol appears in the bottom right corner of the bounding box:

Make the type smaller, or the box bigger, to see all the type.

Hot tip

To resize the type bounding box, select the Horizontal Type tool, click on the Type layer in the Layers panel, then click in the text itself. Drag a resize handle to change the size of the text area.

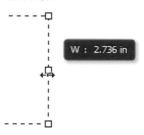

Editing and Selecting Type

To edit type, you must go into text editing mode. To make changes to the character/paragraph formatting of text, you must first highlight or select the text you want to work on. You can then make changes.

Hot tip

If you have any difficulty placing the text insertion point in the text you want to edit, click on the type layer in the Layers panel, to activate the layer first.

Beware

Editable Type layers are represented by the "T" thumbnail in the Layers panel. Double-click the thumbnail to select all the text on a Type layer:

Hot tip

To reposition type, select the Move tool, make sure the Type layer is selected in the Layers panel, then drag the Type layer, as you would to reposition any other layer.

Editing text

1 To edit text, select the Horizontal Type tool. Click directly into the text you want to change. This takes Photoshop into text editing mode. Make changes using the keyboard, as necessary. Click the Commit button in the Options bar to accept the changes you make, and to leave text editing mode. Click the Cancel button in the Options bar if you do not want to keep the changes.

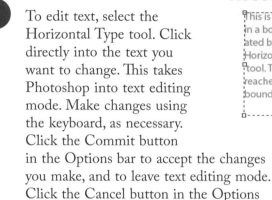

Selecting text

1 Make sure you are in text editing mode, then click and drag across the text to highlight a specific range of characters, from a single character, a word, to all visible text. Double-click on a word to highlight one word. Triple-click to highlight a line of text. Click four times to select a paragraph.

2 In text editing mode, use Ctrl/Command + A to select all text on the layer, or choose Select > All.

3 With the appropriate range of text highlighted, you can then make changes to the settings. The changes you make apply to the highlighted text only.

Character Settings

You can use options in the Options bar when the Type tool is selected, or in the Character panel, to change the settings for selected text.

Font

Use the Font pop-up to choose from the list of fonts available on your system. As you position your cursor on a font name in the list, the selected text changes to show a live preview. Choose a style – such as Bold or Italic – from the Font Style pop-up.

Size

Enter a value in the Size box, to change the size of your type. Points are the default unit of measurement for type in Photoshop.

Leading

Leading controls the distance from one baseline of type to the next. Enter a leading value, in points, in the Leading entry box. Photoshop applies a default leading value of 120% of the type size you have selected, if you leave the leading set to (Auto).

My mother sang while I
was sleeping, rocked me
gentle in the cradle

Kerning and tracking

In the Character panel, you can create settings for kerning and tracking. Metrics, the default, uses the built-in pair kerning table for the font.

 To kern character pairs, click between the characters in the text, to place the text insertion bar. You can enter a value in the Kerning entry box, or use the pop-up to choose a preset value. Negative values move characters closer together. Positive values move characters apart. Press Enter/Return to accept the changes made in the dialog.

You can choose Window > Character to show the Character/Paragraph panel, or you can click the Panels button ( ) in the Options bar, if you have the Type tool selected.

Make sure you select a range of text before you make changes to Character settings.

149

If you are uncertain about which control is which in the Character panel, rest your cursor on the icon to the left of the entry box, until the Tool Tip label appears:

...cont'd

Hot tip

A Faux (or false) style allows you to simulate a font style that doesn't exist on your system. You cannot apply Faux Bold to warped type.

2 For Tracking, highlight a range of text you want to track. Enter a value in the Tracking entry box, or use the pop-up.

# AWAY
Tracking = 84

# AWAY
Tracking = -36

Baseline Shift

The Baseline Shift control allows you to move highlighted characters above or below their original baseline, to create a variety of effects.

Hot tip

To change the color of selected text, click the Color box in the Options bar, or in the Character panel (see pages 63-64 for further information on using the Color Picker).

1 To baseline-shift characters, in text editing mode, make sure you highlight the characters you want to shift.

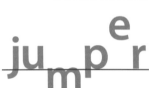

2 Enter a positive value to baseline-shift upwards, enter a negative value to baseline-shift downward.

Anti-aliasing

The anti-aliased setting in the Options bar creates type with a slightly soft edge. It does this by blurring the pixels that form the edge of the type. Use this option to avoid unnecessary jagged edges, unless you are working with very small type. Anti-aliasing text can help the type to blend into its background. Text that is not anti-aliased can look jagged. Choose a level of anti-aliasing from the Anti-alias pop-up in the Options bar.

Type at very small sizes can appear blurred, if anti-aliasing is applied.

None
Sharp
Crisp
Strong
Smooth

Don't forget

You must commit or cancel changes to type before proceeding to make other changes to the image.

Paragraph Settings

The controls in the Paragraph panel are most useful when you are working with Paragraph type consisting of one or more paragraphs. Click the Paragraph panel button, or choose Window > Paragraph if the panel is not already showing.

1 Before you can apply Paragraph settings, you must highlight the range of text on which you want to work (see page 148).

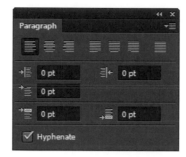

Alignment

1 To change the alignment for selected paragraphs, or a complete layer, click on one of the alignment buttons: Left, Right, Center, in the Paragraph panel or Options bar.

2 Alternatively, choose one of the Justify alignment options to justify type, so that both edges of the column are straight. You cannot justify Point type. The variations for justified type affect how the last line of a paragraph is treated. Rest the cursor on the icon for a Tool Tip label.

Indents

1 To set a Left, Right or First Line indent for selected paragraphs, enter a value in the appropriate entry box.

Space Before, Space After

1 To create additional space above and/or below a paragraph or range of selected paragraphs, enter a value in the Space Before and/or Space After entry boxes.

Select the Type layer in the Layers panel, to apply settings to all paragraphs on that layer.

To set an indent in millimeters, enter a number, followed by mm.

Use the Hyphenate option to allow or disallow hyphenation in selected text:

Masked Type

In essence, the Masked Type option creates a complex selection – a selection in the shape of type. This can be powerful and flexible when you want to show images through the shape of letterforms.

Hot tip

Before you commit it, you can highlight, format, and move mask type as you would standard type.

1 Select the Type Mask tool. Position your cursor on the image where you want the type to start. This sets the text insertion point. A translucent color mask appears across the image.

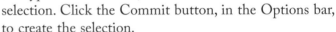

2 Enter text on the keyboard. As you type, the colored mask becomes transparent in the letterforms, to indicate the type mask selection. Click the Commit button, in the Options bar, to create the selection.

Hot tip

After you commit the type mask selection, use one of the selection tools to reposition the selection border, if necessary.

3 A type selection appears in the image window. Notice that the Type Mask tool does not create a new layer.

Don't forget

The Masked Type option creates a selection. You can move, copy, fill or stroke the masked type selection, as you can for any other selection.

4 You can now drag the selection to a new image window, create a new layer from the selection, or use any commands that you would typically use on a selection.

Type and Layer Styles

Layer styles can be applied to type layers, whilst the type layer remains editable.

1 To apply a Layer Style to a type layer, first click on the type layer to make it active.

2 Choose Layer > Layer Styles. Select a style from the style sub-menu. Create settings in the Layer Style dialog box. When you click OK in the dialog box, the layer in the Layers

panel now has a "T" thumbnail and an *fx* icon, indicating that it is an editable type layer with a layer effect applied.

You can also select a layer style, using the Add Layer Style button at the bottom of the Layers panel:

See page 125 for further information on working with layer styles. See page 148 for information on working with editable type layers.

The editable type layer with layer style separated from the background layer.

See Chapter 10, "Paths", for information on creating paths and working with the Pen and Shape tools.

The baseline indicator is the squiggly line that crosses the I-beam three-quarters of the way down the cursor:

To flip type across a path, select the Path Selection tool, or the Direct Selection tool. Position your cursor on the type. When the cursor changes to the I-beam with arrow ( ), click and drag the cursor across the path:

Type Effects

Photoshop provides a variety of creative techniques for producing interesting effects with type.

Type on a path

You can create type that follows a path, created using the Pen tool or a Shape tool.

1 Select the Horizontal or Vertical Type tool. Position your cursor on the path. It is important to position the black arrowhead of the type cursor on the path. Click on the path. Begin typing at the text insertion point. Click the Commit/Cancel button in the Options bar to accept/discard changes. When you commit type on a path, the type appears on a new layer in the Layers panel.

2 To reposition type along the path, select the Path Selection, or Direct Selection tool. Position your cursor at the beginning of the type. When the cursor changes ( ), click and drag to move the type along the path.

Warp Type

Photoshop provides a variety of preset type warps that you can customize to suit your requirements.

1 To warp type, make sure that you have selected a type layer in the Layers panel. Click the Warp Type button ( ) in the Options bar. Choose a warp preset effect, from the Style pop-up menu. Use the Bend, Horizontal and Vertical Distortion sliders to control the effect. Click OK. Warped type remains editable. Choose None, from the Style pop-up menu, to remove warping from a type layer.

10 Paths

Paths are essential for creating cutouts for use in applications, such as Adobe InDesign, and can also be used to create accurate selections.

Converting Selections to Paths

A quick technique for creating a path is to make a selection, convert the selection into a work path, and then into a path.

Hot tip

The Tolerance value controls how closely the path conforms to the selection. A low Tolerance value creates a path that follows the selection tightly, but creates a greater number of points. A high Tolerance value produces a path that follows the selection more loosely, but with fewer points:

1 First make a selection using any of the selection tools. Then, choose Make Work Path, from the Paths panel menu.

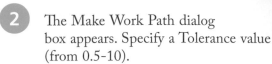
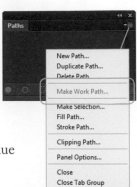

2 The Make Work Path dialog box appears. Specify a Tolerance value (from 0.5-10).

3 Click OK on the dialog box. A work path appears in the Paths panel, along with a thumbnail of the path. The selection disappears. Choose Save Path from the panel menu, if you want to save this path before making any adjustments to it. Enter a name. Click OK in the dialog box. The new path appears in the panel, replacing the work path.

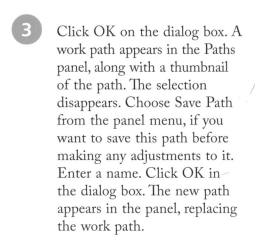

4 To hide the path, click in empty space in the Paths panel. To show the path, click on the path name to select it. The path highlights.

Converting paths to selections
You can also convert a path into a selection. This is useful when you want a very accurate selection.

Don't forget

You can only have one work path in the Paths panel at any one time. A work path is a temporary path only. For a path to be saved when you save your file, you must first save the path.

1 To convert a path into a selection, click on the path in the Paths panel to highlight it. Then choose Make Selection from the panel menu, or click the Load Path as Selection button.

Using the Pen Tool

You can use the Pen tool to create paths. When you start to create a path, it appears as a "work path" in the Paths panel. A work path is only a temporary path.

The Pen tool creates anchor points, which are connected by straight lines or curved segments. You can use the other tools in the Paths tool group to modify a path by adding, deleting, or moving anchor points, and by changing the nature of the point, from smooth to corner, and vice versa. You can also edit curved segments by dragging the Bézier direction points.

Use the Paths panel menu (▾≣) to create a new path, before you use the Pen tool to automatically save the path, without going through the intermediary stage of a work path.

1 To create a path, select the Pen tool in the Tool panel. Select the Path option from the Tool Mode pop-up in the Options bar. You can select the Rubber Band option from the Settings pop-up (⚙)in the Options bar, to see a preview of the line segments as you draw.

As you are creating a path, you can press the Delete key to delete the last anchor point. Press Delete twice to delete the entire path.

2 Position your cursor where you want to start drawing the path, then click, release the button, move the mouse, and click again to create a straight line segment. Continue moving your cursor, and clicking to create further straight line segments.

3 Alternatively, you can click and drag to set an anchor point, and create direction lines for a curve segment. Then, release the button and move the cursor, and click and drag again to create the next anchor point with direction lines. Continue in this way to create the path you want. Position the Pen tool cursor at the start point. Notice that the cursor now has a small circle attached to it. Click to create a closed path. The path appears in the Paths panel, with the default title of Work Path.

Use the Freeform Pen tool to create a path, by clicking and dragging the mouse. This is similar to drawing with a pencil. You have no control over where Photoshop places anchor points, but you can easily edit the path after it is drawn.

...cont'd

You can only have one work path in a file. It is a good idea to save the path and give it a name, so you do not delete it accidentally by creating another work path. See page 156 for details on saving your work path.

Hot tip

Select Auto Add/Delete in the Options bar, to use the Pen tool to add and delete anchor points for a selected path. The tool cursor changes intelligently, depending on whether you position the cursor on an anchor point or a line segment.

Beware

The paths in these illustrations are positioned away from the object, so that they display more clearly. When you create a clipping path, it is best to position the path a pixel or so inside the shape you want to cut out, to avoid including unwanted edge pixels.

4. To create an open path, follow the techniques outlined in steps 1-3, but instead of clicking back at the start point, click on the Pen tool in the Tool panel to finish the path. This is now an 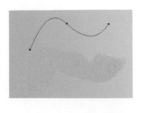 open path, to which you could, for example, apply a stroke.

Creating corner points

As you use the Pen tool to create paths, you can draw corner points as you go, in combination with straight line segments and smooth points. In many instances, smooth points alone cannot create the shape of the path you want.

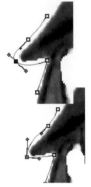

A corner point allows a sharp change of direction at the anchor point. In a corner point, the direction points can be manipulated independently. This is what makes them essential to create paths that require sharp changes of direction.

1. To draw a corner point, click and drag as you would to set a smooth point. Concentrate on getting the shape of the path coming into the point correct. Do not release the mouse button.

2. Hold down Alt/option, then drag the direction point. This converts the point to a corner point. You are now controlling the direction of the outgoing curve segment. As you drag the second direction point, notice that it no longer has any effect on the incoming direction point. Release the mouse button.

3. Move your cursor to a new position, then continue drawing either smooth or corner points.

Selecting Paths and Points

Use the following techniques for selecting, deselecting, and deleting paths.

1 To select a path, first you have to show it. To do this, click the path entry in the Paths panel. The path now shows in the image window.

2 To select and move an entire path, select the Path Selection tool, and then click anywhere on the path. All anchor points on the path highlight as solid squares. Drag an anchor point, or any part of the selected path to reposition it. To deselect a path, click away from the path using the Path Selection tool. The path still shows, but is not selected.

A selected anchor point is a solid square; a non-selected point is a hollow square.

3 To select and edit anchor points, and their associated direction points, select the Direct Selection tool. Click on a visible, but not selected, path to make it active. You now see the curve and line segments that form the path together with the anchor points.

4 Click on the anchor point of a curve segment to select the point. The anchor point you click on becomes solid, and it displays its direction points.

To improve the clarity of these illustrations, the path has been moved away from the edge of the image.

5 To delete a path using the Direct Selection tool, with a point or line segment of the path selected, press Delete twice. Alternatively, select the entire path using the Path Selection tool, then press Delete. You can also drag the path name onto the Trash can icon, in the Paths panel.

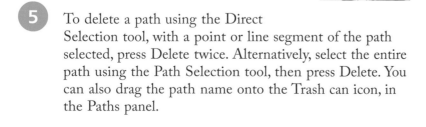

Managing Points

To achieve a precise path, you often need to add, delete, and convert points on a path.

Don't forget

For a smooth point, when you drag one of the direction points in a circular direction, using the Direct Selection tool, the other point balances it to maintain a smooth curve at the anchor point.

Don't forget

A corner point is one that allows a sharp change of direction at the anchor point. Notice that, for a corner point, when you drag one of the direction points, the other point is not affected – you have complete, independent control over each direction point.

Beware

The Add Anchor Point tool cursor appears as a hollow arrow, until you position it on a path. It then becomes the Pen cursor, with an additional plus (+) symbol. Similarly, the Delete Anchor Point tool cursor appears only when you position the cursor on an existing anchor point.

1 To add a point, make sure the path is selected, select the Add Anchor Point tool from the Pen Tool group, position your cursor on the path, and then click. If you click on a curve or straight line segment, you automatically get an anchor point with direction points.

2 To delete a point, make sure the path is selected, select the Delete Anchor Point tool, position your cursor on an existing anchor point, then click. The path redraws without the point.

3 To convert a smooth point into a corner point, select an anchor point, with the Direct Selection tool. Select the Convert Point tool, position your cursor on a direction point, then click and drag. Use the Direct Selection tool to make any further changes to the direction points.

4 To convert anchor points on straight line segments into smooth points, select the Convert Point tool, position your cursor on the anchor point, then click and drag. Direction lines appear around the point. Use the Direct Selection tool to make any further changes to the points.

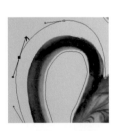

5 To convert a smooth point into a corner point, without direction lines, select the Convert Point tool, then click on an anchor point.

Manipulating Points

Paths invariably need to be modified and fine-tuned to produce the result you require.

1 To edit a smooth point, make sure the path is selected, then, using the Direct Selection tool, click on the anchor point to select it. Direction points appear either side of the anchor point. Direction points control the shape and length of a curve segment.

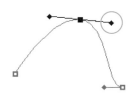

2 When you drag a direction point of a smooth anchor point, as you change the angle of one side, the other direction point moves to balance the point you are moving. This ensures the curve is always smooth through the anchor point.

3 The further away from the anchor point you drag a direction point, the longer the associated curve segment becomes. As the curve segment is anchored at the anchor points at either end, this causes the curve segment to bow out more. Bring the direction point closer to the anchor point, and the curve segment becomes shorter.

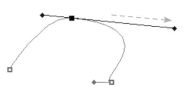

4 When you drag direction points on a corner anchor point, each moves totally independently of the other, allowing a sharp change of direction at the point.

Select the Direct Selection tool to edit paths and points (see page 159, "Selecting Paths and Points").

Select an anchor point, and press the arrow keys to move the selected point in one pixel increments.

With the Pen tool selected, hold down Ctrl/Command to temporarily toggle to the Direct Selection tool. When the cursor is positioned directly over an anchor point, or direction point, hold down Alt/option to toggle to the Convert Point tool.

Exporting Paths

Exporting paths to Adobe Illustrator

Sometimes it is useful to export a path from Photoshop into Adobe Illustrator, to perform further manipulation on it.

1 To export a path to Adobe Illustrator, make sure you have a saved path in the Paths panel.

2 Choose File > Export > Paths to Illustrator. In the Export Paths to File dialog box, if your Photoshop document has more than one saved path, use the Paths pop-up to choose the path you want to export. Click OK.

3 Specify where you want to save the file, in the Choose File Name dialog box. Click Save.

4 Use File > Open in Adobe Illustrator, to import the path. If the path is not visible initially, use the Selection tool to marquee select within the artboard, then apply a fill or stroke to the selected path.

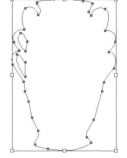

5 See pages 34-35 for information on placing an Illustrator EPS into Photoshop.

Hot tip

You can also copy a selected path from Photoshop into Illustrator. For greatest flexibility when you paste the path in Illustrator, select the Compound Shape (fully editable) option:

Smart Guides

Smart Guides make it easy to draw, manipulate and position objects, shapes and layers with pin-point accuracy without the need for additional ruler guides.

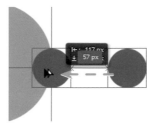

1 Working with the Move tool, if you hold down the Alt/ option to key as you drag the contents of a layer, temporary, interactive readout panels and measurement guides (light magenta) appear to assist accurate positioning of the duplicate layer.

2 Smart Guides appear to indicate equal spacing between objects as you duplicate and reposition layers.

Working with the Move tool, hold down Alt/ option to create a copy of a layer as you press and drag the mouse.

3 Select a target layer. Working with the Move tool, hover your cursor over another, unselected layer (don't click on it or attempt to drag it). Then, hold down Ctrl/Command to display measurements indicating the relationship of objects on the target layer and the "hover over" layer. Use the arrow keys on your keyboard to nudge the contents of the target layer.

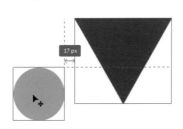

4 Working with the Move tool, position your cursor away from the object/pixels on the selected, target layer. Then, hold down Ctrl/ Command to display Smart Guides indicating distances to each edge of the canvas.

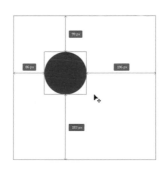

Creating Shape Layers

The Shape tools allow you to create lines, rectangles, and ovals, as well as polygons and custom shapes. Use the Options bar to set specific options for each tool individually.

1 To draw a rectangle as a shape layer, select the Rectangle tool. Make sure you select Shape from the Pick tool mode pop-up menu in the Options bar. Use the Fill pop-up panel in the Options bar to select a color if you want the rectangle to appear with a fill as soon as you draw it.

Hot tip

Use the Settings pop-up menu (⚙) in the Options bar to set specific options for tools, if required. For example, you can add arrowheads to lines:

2 Position your cursor in the image window. Drag diagonally to define the size of the shape. A new shape layer appears in the Layers panel. Use controls in the Options bar to create settings for the shape. To create additional shapes on the same shape layer, either choose a new shape tool from the Tool panel, or use the same tool, but hold down Shift as you start to drag to define the new shape.

Hot tip

To draw a square, hold down Shift, then drag with the Rectangle tool. Release the mouse button before you release Shift, otherwise the constraint effect will be lost. Hold down Alt/ option, then drag with the Rectangle tool to draw a rectangle from the center out. You can use the same modifier keys with the Ellipse tool to create circles.

3 When you create a shape using the Rectangle, Rounded Rectangle and Ellipse tools, the Live Shape Properties panel also appears. (See next page for details.)

4 With a shape layer selected, use the Direct Selection tool to select and make changes to the shape of the object in the image window. If you edit a Live Shape, a prompt appears to indicate that the shape will become a path if you proceed – you will no longer be able to access its Live Shape Properties.

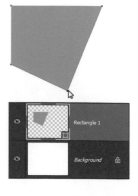

Fill and Stroke for Shapes

When working with shape layers, you can apply a varied and flexible range of fill and stroke attributes using controls in the Options bar, and the Live Shape Properties panel for Rectangles and Ellipses.

Use fill settings to color the inside of the shape you draw. You can apply solid, gradient and pattern fills to shape layers. A stroke is a visible outline around the edge of the shape. You can apply solid colors, gradients and patterns to the stroke, and you can also specify the thickness of the stroke and apply dashed or dotted styles.

Click the None button if you want to remove a fill from a shape layer.

1 When you create a shape layer, the new shape immediately takes on any fill and stroke settings currently set in the Options bar.

2 To change the fill color for the active shape layer, click on the Set fill type pop-up in the Options bar or the Live Shape Properties panel to show the Fill type panel.

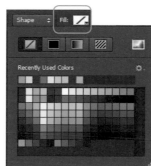

When you draw a shape using the Rectangle, Rounded Rectangle or Ellipse tool, the Live Shape Properties panel appears:

3 Use the top row of buttons to specify whether you want a solid, gradient or pattern fill (see page 79 for information on working with gradients and page 80 for information on working with patterns).

4 To apply a solid fill color, click the Solid Color button, then click on one of the preset colors in the swatches panel, or click one of the Recently Used color swatches. You can click the Color Picker button (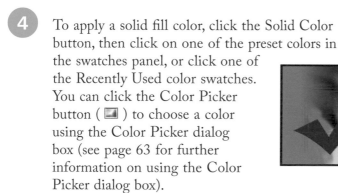) to choose a color using the Color Picker dialog box (see page 63 for further information on using the Color Picker dialog box).

Double-click the Shape Layer thumbnail in the Layers panel, to change the fill color using the Color Picker dialog box.

5 After you select a fill color, click the Fill pop-up triangle again to close the Fill Type panel.

165

...cont'd

Working with Strokes

Hot tip

For rectangles, use the corner controls in the Live Shape Properties panel to create settings for rounded corners:

Don't forget

Click the None button in the Set stroke type panel if you want to remove a stroke from a shape layer.

Hot tip

To create your own custom dashed or dotted stroke styles, click the More Options button at the bottom of the Stroke Options dialog box:

More Options...

1 Make sure that you still have a shape tool selected, the shape layer is active, and that the Pick tool mode pop-up remains set to Shape. You can create the settings you want in the Options bar and, for rectangles and ellipses, also in the Live Shape Properties panel.

2 Either, enter a value for stroke weight in the Set stroke width entry field, or drag the slider to change the stroke weight. The stroke color defaults to black.

3 Use the Set stroke type pop-up to specify a solid, gradient or pattern stroke. To apply a solid stroke color, click the Solid Color button, then click on a color box in the swatches panel, or click one of the Recently Used color boxes. Click the Color Picker button ( ) to choose a color using the Color Picker dialog box.

4 Click the Set stroke style pop-up, then click one of the preset options to change the stroke from solid to a dashed or dotted stroke.

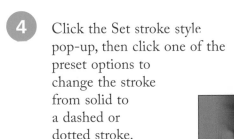

11 Channels and Masks

Channels and masks bring

powerful, creative capabilities

for protecting parts of an

image, fully or partially, from

editing you perform on the

unmasked areas.

Hot tip

You can make a rough selection first, then go into Quick Mask mode and edit the mask further, if necessary.

Beware

Painting with gray, or any other color, creates a semi-transparent or partial mask.

Quick Mask Mode

In Quick Mask mode, you create a 50% red, semi-transparent overlay. This overlay represents the protected area of the image. The overlay is similar in concept to a traditional Rubylith mask. Quick Mask mode is particularly useful, because you can see both the image and the mask as you create and fine-tune the mask.

1 To create a quick mask, click the Edit in Quick Mask Mode button in the Tool panel. Make sure that the default foreground and background colors are black and white, respectively.

2 Show the Brushes panel and choose a brush size. Use a hard-edged brush to create selections with a clearly defined edge. Use a soft-edged brush to create selections that are slightly softer along the edge. Select a painting tool and drag across your image to "paint" in the mask. Painting with black adds to the mask. Although you see through the 50% red mask, the pixels covered by the mask are completely protected.

3 To remove areas from the mask, you can use the Eraser tool, or paint with white.

4 When you are satisfied with your mask, click the Edit in Standard Mode button. This turns the areas of the image that were not part of your quick mask into a selection. You can now make changes to the selected areas (in this example on the left, the Lens Blur filter has been applied), leaving the areas that were quick 'masked' unchanged.

The Channels Panel

The Channels panel (Window > Channels) shows a breakdown of the color components that combine to make up the composite color image you work with most of the time on-screen.

For example, in RGB mode, there are four channels – the composite image (all the other channels combined), and then a channel each for the red, green and blue color components of the image. In CMYK mode, there are five channels.

Using the Channels panel, you can be selective about which of the color components you change in your image.

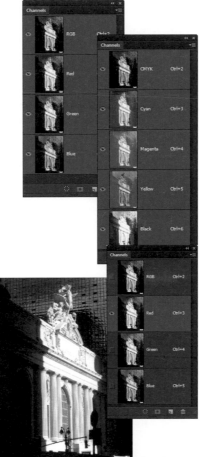

1 To switch to a specific channel, click the channel name in the Channels panel. The channel highlights to indicate that it is selected. The image window changes according to the channel you chose.

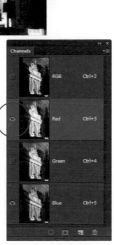

2 You can view additional channels by clicking the Visibility button for a channel. The image window changes, but your editing remains limited to the selected channel.

3 Click on the composite RGB channel to return to normal image-editing view.

169

Hot tip

You can change the display of channels, from grayscale to the color they represent, by choosing Edit > Preferences > Interface (Windows), or Photoshop > Preferences > Interface (Mac). Select the Show Channels in Color checkbox:

☑ Enable Floating Document V
☐ Show Channels in Color
Show Transformation Values

Beware

Indexed Color mode, Grayscale mode, and Bitmap mode all have only one channel.

Save and Load Selections

Because you can only have one "active" selection in an image at any one time, the facility to store a selection, which can be reloaded later, is vital, especially if the selection is complex and took some time to create. You save selections as an extra channel in the Channels panel. These extra channels are referred to as "alpha channels".

Saving selections

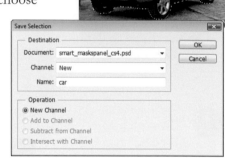

1 To save a selection to a channel, make your selection on the image, then choose Select > Save Selection. The Save Selection dialog box appears. Specify in which document you wish to save the channel (you can save channels in another document to keep the file size of the current document as small as possible). Leave the Channel pop-up on New. Enter a name for the channel. Click OK. Alternatively, make your selection and then click the Save Selection as Channel button in the Channels panel.

2 An additional channel appears in the Channels panel. This is the new "alpha channel". An alpha channel is a grayscale channel.

3 When you have saved a selection to an alpha channel, you can freely deselect the selection in your image, as you can now reselect the exact same area at any time, using the alpha channel.

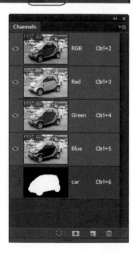

An alpha channel is an 8-bit grayscale channel, which means that every time you save a selection as a channel, you are adding to the file size of your image.

File formats that can retain alpha channel information when you save include: Photoshop, PDF, PICT and TIFF.

When you are working in Quick Mask mode, you can turn the quick mask into an alpha channel by dragging the quick mask entry, which appears in the Channels panel, onto the New Channel button:

Loading selections

Use the following process to reselect an area using the alpha channel.

1 To load a channel as a selection on the image, make sure the composite image is displayed. You can do this by clicking on the topmost channel name in the Channels panel. Then choose Select > Load Selection. The Load Selection dialog box appears.

You can display an alpha channel without loading it onto the image as a selection. You can then edit the mask by painting with black, white, or gray.

In the Channels panel, click on the alpha channel you want to display.

2 Use the Channel pop-up menu to specify which channel you want to load. Select an operation,

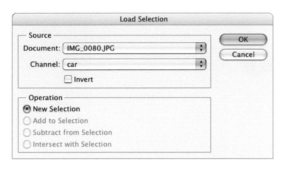

The white area represents the selection, and the black portions represent the protected areas.

as appropriate. The operations allow you to control how the selection you are about to load interacts with any existing selection in the image – adding to it, subtracting from it, or intersecting with it. Click OK.

Paint with black to remove areas from the selection mask. Paint with white on any black portion of the mask to add it to the selection:

3 Alternatively, using the Channels panel, drag the channel you want to load onto the Load Selection icon.

4 To delete a channel, drag the channel name onto the Trash can icon at the bottom of the panel.

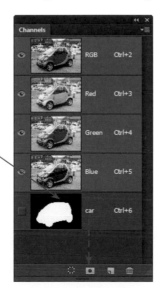

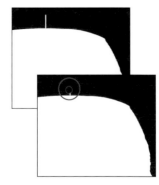

Layer Masks

Use layer masks to hide or reveal areas of a layer. A layer mask is extremely useful, because you can use it to try out effects without actually changing the pixels on the layer. When you have achieved the result you want, you can apply the mask as a permanent change. If you are not satisfied, you can discard the mask without having permanently affected the pixels on the layer.

For information on creating layers, see Chapter 8. For information on using filters, see Chapter 13.

This example begins with an image with two layers. The original Background layer, and another layer created using the Render > Fibres filter positioned above it.

1 To create a layer mask for the fibres layer, first click on the layer to make it active. Choose Layer > Layer Mask > Reveal All. Reveal All makes all the pixels on the layer visible. The fibres layer now completely obscures the Background layer.

You can add a Reveal All layer mask to a selected layer by clicking the Add Layer Mask button ( ), at the bottom of the Layers panel. Alt + click the button to add a Hide All layer mask.

2 In the Layers panel, the layer mask is active, indicated by the highlight border on the mask thumbnail. Click on the layer thumbnail if you want to make the layer active. Click on the Layer Mask thumbnail to continue editing the mask.

3 With the layer mask thumbnail selected, make sure that the foreground color is set to black. Choose a painting tool and start painting. Painting with black hides pixels on the fibres layer, revealing pixels on the Background layer below it.

4 Pixels on the fibres layer are not permanently erased when you paint with black. Paint with white to show pixels on the fibres layer – in effect, hiding pixels on the Background layer. (If you choose Layer > Add Layer Mask > Hide All, you start with the opposite scenario to the above. Now all the pixels on the fibres layer are hidden. Paint with white to reveal pixels on the fibres layer, paint with black to hide them.)

You can paint with shades of gray, to partially hide pixels on the fibres layer.

5 To temporarily switch off the layer mask, choose Layer > Layer Mask > Disable, or hold down Shift, then click on the Layer Mask thumbnail. To reactivate the mask, choose Layer > Layer Mask > Enable, or hold down Shift, then click again on the Layer Mask thumbnail.

6 To apply the layer mask as a permanent change, choose Layer > Layer Mask > Apply.

7 To discard the layer mask, without affecting pixels on the layer, choose Layer > Layer Mask > Delete. Or drag the Layer Mask thumbnail (not the Layer thumbnail) onto the Trash can icon in the bottom of the panel. Click Apply or Delete. Once you apply a layer mask, you lose the flexibility of making further changes – the effect is fixed. Click Delete only if you want to discard the mask.

Once you understand the principles of using layer masks, the Mask Properties panel provides quick and convenient access to controls for manipulating and fine-tuning layer masks (see pages 174–176).

Pixel and Vector Masks

The Mask Properties panel provides a convenient, streamlined approach to manipulating layer masks, with its range of flexible, easy-to-access set of controls. Work with the Mask Properties panel in conjunction with the Layers panel.

Pixel Masks

Pixel masks are layer masks – you can paint with Black or White, or shades of gray, to hide or show the pixels in the masks. The result is to selectively reveal or hide the image content on layers below.

Beware

If you apply a layer mask to the Background layer, Photoshop automatically converts the layer to "Layer 0", as you cannot create a layer or vector mask on the default Background layer.

1 To create a pixel layer mask, make sure you select the layer you want to use as the mask, then click the Add layer mask button (■) at the bottom of the Layers panel. A layer mask thumbnail appears to the right of the layer thumbnail.

Layer mask thumbnail

Beware

When you start to work with layer and vector masks, it is important that you distinguish between the layer thumbnail, which appears on the left, and the layer mask or vector mask thumbnail, which appears to the right of the layer thumbnail:

Layer mask thumbnail

2 In the image window, paint with White, Black, or shades of gray to hide or reveal the pixels that form the mask. Paint with a Black to White gradient, as in the example below, to create a gradual transition that hides or reveals the pixels in the mask.

Hot tip

Click the Apply Mask button (■) in the Properties panel when you have finished making changes to the mask, and you want to make changes permanent. You will no longer be able to edit and manipulate the mask.

3 To further manipulate and fine-tune the mask, click the Properties button to show the Mask Properties panel. Use

Density, Feather, Mask Edge, Color Range, and Invert settings in the Properties panel to fine tune the mask to meet your requirements (see page 176 for details).

Vector Masks

Vector masks use a precisely-defined vector shape to create the mask. As with a pixel mask, you use the shape to selectively reveal or hide image content on the layers below.

1 To create a vector mask, make sure you select the layer you want to mask in the layers panel. In the image window, either use the Pen tool, or one of the Shape tools, to draw a vector path.

2 Choose Layers > Vector Mask > Current Path (the path does not need to be selected) to create the vector mask. Alternatively, after you draw the vector path, hold down Ctrl/Command then click the Add layer mask button ( ) at the bottom of the Layers panel. A vector mask thumbnail appears to the right of the layer thumbnail. The vector path reveals pixels on the layer that fall inside the path, and hides those that fall outside: effectively creating areas of transparency on the outside of the path.

3 Although a vector mask uses precise mathematical curves to define the mask, you can use the Density and Feather sliders to further control the appearance of the mask in the Properties panel.

You create a Vector mask using a Shape tool, or the Pen tool. Vector masks typically have sharp, clearly defined edges, but you can use the Feather slider in the Properties panel to soften and blur a vector mask, if desired.

To further control the appearance of a vector mask, make sure the vector mask thumbnail is active, then click the Properties button ( ) to show the Properties panel for the mask:

Mask Properties Panel

Use the controls in the Properties panel to modify and refine a mask, to achieve the desired result.

Density slider

The Density slider allows you to control the opacity of the layer mask – effectively making the mask semi-transparent. Adjusting mask density can help create subtle blending effects in images.

Feather Slider

Use the Feather slider to soften and blur the mask non-destructively.

Mask Edge

Click the Mask Edge button to access the Refine Mask dialog box. This dialog box gives you a powerful and flexible set of controls, which you can use to fine-tune the pixels that form the edge of the mask region. The controls are the same as in the Refine Edge dialog box – see page 105 for further information.

Color Range

The Color Range command allows you to create complex layer masks, based on ranges of similar colors in the image.

1 With the layer mask active, click the Color Range button. In the Color Range dialog box, select the Image radio button to set the preview in the dialog box, then select an option from the Selection Preview, Grayscale, for example to set the preview in the image window.

2 Click in the preview box with the Eyedropper tool to begin selecting colors. Use the fuzziness slider to increase or decrease the range of similar colors that are included in the mask. Use the Add to/ Subtract from Sample eyedroppers to increase or reduce the number of colors in the mask.

Don't forget

One of the main reasons for using layer masks is to work on images non-destructively – until you either apply or discard the mask, you can continue to adjust settings to achieve the effect you want.

Hot tip

Click the Invert button to reverse the layer mask – black areas of the mask become white, and vice versa. What the mask previously revealed is hidden, and what was previously hidden becomes visible.

Hot tip

Switch on the Localized Color Clusters to limit the selection of colors to pixels that are inside the fuzziness threshold and adjacent, then use the Range slider to expand or spread the cluster area, if necessary.

12 Color Adjustments

Color correction involves making changes to the overall brightness and contrast, and also the color balance in an image, to compensate for any tonal deficiencies and color casts in the original.

Brightness/Contrast

The Brightness/Contrast command provides the least complicated controls for changing overall brightness/contrast levels in an image. It does not change individual color channels; it makes the same adjustment to all pixels across the full tonal range of the image.

Hot tip

Click the Preview button in the Brightness/Contrast dialog box to see, on-screen, the result of the settings you choose, as you make the changes.

Beware

For images created in a previous version of Photoshop, the Use Legacy option is automatically selected, if you work with a Brightness/Contrast adjustment layer. Use of Legacy is not recommended for high quality printed output, as "clipping", or loss of detail, can occur in highlights or shadows.

178

1 To change brightness and contrast for an entire image, or for a selection, choose Image > Adjustments > Brightness/ Contrast. Drag the Brightness and Contrast sliders, or enter values in the entry boxes. Click OK in the dialog box.

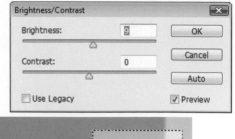

2 Choose Image > Auto Contrast to automatically adjust the contrast for an image or selection. Highlights should appear lighter, and shadows darker, giving an overall improvement to the image. Auto Contrast does not adjust individual channels. It makes highlights appear lighter and shadows darker by mapping the lightest and darkest pixels in the image to white and black, respectively.

Hot tip

Click the Brightness/ Contrast button ( ) in the Adjustments panel to set up a Brightness/ Contrast adjustment layer. Adjustment layers allow you to make "non-destructive" edits to an image. (See pages 186-187.)

Auto Tone and Auto Color

Auto Tone allows you to adjust brightness and contrast automatically. Auto Tone examines each color channel independently, and changes the darkest pixels to black and the lightest pixels to white, then redistributes the remaining shades of gray between these two points.

Auto Tone works best on images that have a reasonably even distribution of tonal values throughout the image, as it redistributes pixels based on white and black points, with a tendency to increase contrast.

Auto Color removes unwanted color casts in an image, without adjusting the contrast in an image.

1. To apply Auto Tone to an image, choose Image > Auto Tone. (Use Edit > Undo if the result is not satisfactory.)

2. To apply Auto Color to an image, choose Image > Auto Color. (Use Edit > Undo if the result is not satisfactory.)

You can also use the Auto Tone command from within the Levels and Curves dialog boxes. Click the Auto button.

Auto Tone adjusts each color channel in the image individually. As a result, it may remove or sometimes introduce color casts.

179

Original   Auto Tone   Auto Color

Both Auto Tone and Auto Color generally produce good results on RGB images, but they do not allow the precision of the manual adjustments, which you can make by using the Levels and Curves dialog boxes or adjustment layers.

The Levels Dialog Box

Use the Levels dialog box (Image > Adjustments > Levels) to adjust the tonal balance for color and grayscale images. You can adjust highlight, shadow, and midtone ranges for a selection, or for an entire image, or you can make changes to individual channels only.

Input Levels

The Input Levels sliders and entry boxes allow you to improve the contrast in a "flat" image.

1 Use the Channel pop-up menu to select a channel. If you do not select an individual channel, you can work on the composite image, and affect all channels.

2 To darken an image, drag the solid black slider to the right. Alternatively, enter an appropriate value in the leftmost Input Levels entry box. This maps pixels to black. For example, if you drag the black slider to 15, all pixels with an original value between 0 and 15 become black. The result is a darker image.

The most flexible way of working with Levels, Curves, and Color Balance is to set up Adjustment layers (see pages 186-187). Adjustment layers allow you to repeatedly adjust settings in the respective dialog boxes, until you are satisfied with the result.

The spiky graph in the middle of the Levels dialog box is a Histogram. See pages 184-185 for an explanation of the Histogram in the Levels dialog box.

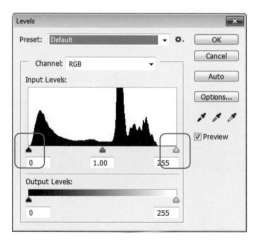

3 To lighten an image, drag the hollow, white Input Levels slider to the left. Alternatively, enter an appropriate value in the rightmost Input Levels entry box. The result is to map pixels to white. For example, if you drag the white slider to 245, all pixels with an original value between 245 and 255 become white. The result is a lighter image.

Dragging either, or both, of the black or white Input Levels sliders inwards has the effect of increasing contrast in the image.

180

Gamma

The gray triangle and the middle Input Levels entry box controls the Gamma value in the image. The Gamma value is the brightness level of mid-gray pixels in the image.

1 To lighten midtones, drag the gray slider to the left, or increase the Gamma value in the Input Levels entry box, above the default setting of 1.00.

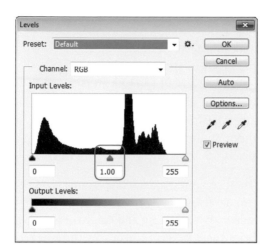

Preset levels adjustments are available in the Presets pop-up menu. If you create your own settings in the Levels dialog box that you want to reuse, select Save Preset from the panel menu (✿.). Specify a name and location for the preset. The saved preset becomes available in the Presets pop-up menu.

2 To darken midtones, drag the gray slider to the right, or decrease the Gamma value in the Input Levels entry box.

See page 179 for an explanation of Auto Tone and the Auto button.

Output Levels

You can use the Output Levels entry boxes or sliders to decrease the amount of contrast in an image. Typically, you do this to target highlight and shadow values, to match the output capabilities of a particular printing press, with the aim of preserving highlight and shadow detail.

1 Drag the black Output Levels slider to the right to lighten the image, and to reduce the contrast.

2 Drag the white Output Levels slider to the left to darken the image, and to reduce the contrast.

For RGB and CMYK images, use the Channels pop-up menu to make tonal adjustments to individual channels. Work with a calibrated monitor to ensure consistent and predictable results.

181

The Curves Dialog Box

The Curves dialog box (Image > Adjustments > Curves) offers the most versatile set of controls for making tonal adjustments in an image. The central brightness graph in the dialog box displays the original and adjusted brightness values for pixels in the image. The graph is a straight line from 0 (black) to 255 (white) before any adjustments are made – input and output values for pixels are the same.

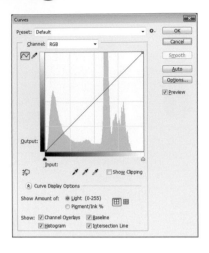

The horizontal axis of the graph represents the original or input values, the vertical axis represents the output or adjusted values. By adjusting the brightness curve, you are remapping the brightness values of pixels in the image.

Beware

For RGB images, the default brightness bar along the bottom edge of the graph starts black and graduates to white. In this state, the brightness curve indicates the brightness values of colors in the image; the brightness curve starts at 0, for black, and moves to 255, for white.

Click the Curve Display Options button (⊗), then select the Pigment/Ink % radio button to reverse the display.

1 To add a point to the curve, make sure the Point tool is selected (you can add up to 14 points). Click on the curve. Drag the point(s) around to edit the curve. Or click above or below the graph to adjust the curve, according to where you clicked.

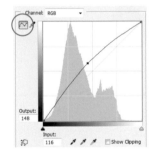

2 To delete a point, click on a point to select it, then press the Delete/Backspace key. You can also drag it outside the Brightness graph.

Hot tip

Click the Curve Display Options button (⊗), then use the Simple/Detailed Grid buttons to display gridlines in 25% or 10% increments, respectively:

3 To lighten or darken an image, select the Point tool, position your cursor near the midpoint of the graph, then click to place a new point. Click and drag this point upwards to lighten, downwards to darken.

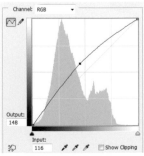

...cont'd

4 To increase the contrast in an image, place a point at roughly the ¼ tone part of the graph, and drag this upwards to lighten the highlights. Next, place a point at roughly the ¾ tone part of the graph. Drag this downward to darken the

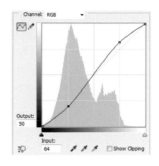

shadow areas. The result is an increase in the contrast in the image, by lightening the highlights and darkening the shadows, whilst leaving the midtones more or less untouched. You can also select the Increase Contrast preset from the Preset pop-up, to achieve a similar effect.

5 Reverse the setting in step 4 to decrease the contrast in an image.

6 To limit changes to the midtones and highlights, click on the graph to place a point at the ¾ tone. Place a point at the ¼ tone and drag this upwards. Reverse this procedure to change midtones and shadows without affecting highlights.

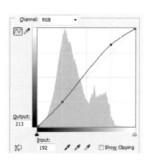

7 Move the black point/white point sliders inwards to increase the overall contrast in an image, as you can do in the Levels dialog box (see pages 180-181 for further information). Deselect Histogram in the Curve Display options to hide the histogram.

8 Click the Curve Display Options expand button to reveal further options for controlling the appearance of the dialog box, as you change settings.

Hold down Alt/option, then click on the Reset button (previously Cancel) to restore the original settings in the dialog box.

Select a point on the graph, then press the arrow keys on your keyboard to move the point in increments.

183

Use the Channels pop-up to edit the baseline curve for individual color channels. It is important to work with a calibrated monitor, to accurately assess the impact of changes you make to individual color channels. With Channel Overlays selected in Curve Display Options, changes to individual color channels are visible in the composite brightness graph.

The Histogram Panel

A histogram is a bar chart that represents the distribution of pixels in an image. Shadows are on the left side of the histogram, highlights on the right, and midtones in the middle. The spread of pixels through the shadows, midtones, and highlights represents the tonal balance in an image.

Having the Histogram panel visible as you work on an image can help you evaluate the effect of the changes and adjustments you make.

Don't forget

In a histogram, the horizontal axis plots color or luminosity levels, from 0–255. The vertical axis plots the number of pixels at each level.

1 Choose Window > Histogram to show the panel. The Histogram panel is initially grouped with the Navigator panel. The Histogram panel opens in Compact View, but you can expand it to show statistical information and histograms for color channels.

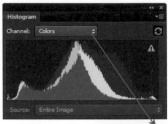

2 Choose Expanded View from the Histogram panel menu ( ), to enable access to the Channel pop-up menu. Choose from Red, Green, Blue, Luminosity, and Colors, to view the histogram for the channel you specify. For an image with more than one layer you can choose Selected Layer from the Source drop-down menu, to view a histogram for the pixel content on the currently active layer.

Hot tip

Choose Show Channels in Color, from the panel menu, to display colored histograms for the Red, Green, and Blue channels.

3 For RGB and CMYK images, you can choose Luminosity from the Channel pop-up menu to display a luminosity channel only.

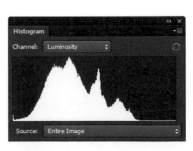

4 To show statistical information for the histogram, choose Show Statistics from the Histogram panel menu. Move your cursor through the bars of the histogram itself to get readouts for Level, Count, and Percentile, in the statistics area.

When in All Channels view, choosing an option from the Channels drop down menu changes the top histogram only.

5 Choose All Channels View to display an extended panel, with histograms for all channels in the image, with the exception of Alpha channels, Spot channels, and masks. The topmost histogram represents the luminance, or overall brightness values, for the composite channel. Select Show Channels in Color from the panel menu, to display color channels in color.

When working in dialog boxes, such as Levels and Curves, provided that the Preview option is selected, the Histogram panel updates as you make changes to the settings in the dialog box.

6 The Cached Data warning icon (▲) appears when the Histogram panel display is based on information held in cache (an area of short-term memory), rather than the actual current state of the image. To ensure that the histogram represents all pixels in the image, in their current state, either click the Cached Data warning icon, or click the Uncached Refresh button (⟳). Photoshop uses cached information for the image, in order to display information in the histogram quickly, but slightly less accurately, as the cached information is based on a representative sampling of pixels in the image only.

185

The Adjustments Panel

Using an adjustment layer on an image is like positioning a lens above the pixels on the layers below it to change their appearance. If you don't like the result, you can edit the adjustment layer to achieve the result you want, or you can discard it. When you are satisfied with the result, you can implement the adjustment layer as a permanent change.

The most efficient way to create adjustment layers is through the Adjustments panel. You can edit settings for the adjustment layer using the Properties panel.

Don't forget

As in previous versions of Photoshop, you can also apply adjustment layers by choosing Layers > New Adjustment Layer, then selecting an adjustment layer type from the sub-menu.

1 Click the Adjustments tab in the Panel dock, if necessary, to show the Adjustments panel. Rest your cursor on an icon to see the name of the adjustment as a tool tip and along the top of the panel.

186

Don't forget

An adjustment layer is created above the currently active layer. Its settings apply to the layers below it and do not affect layers above.

2 Select a layer in the Layers panel, as adjustment layers are created above the currently active layer. Click on an adjustment layer button to reveal the Properties panel which displays controls for the adjustment layer. As soon as you click on an adjustment button, an adjustment layer appears in the Layers panel, automatically named according to the type of adjustment you selected.

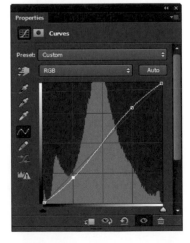

Hot tip

By reducing the Opacity setting for an adjustment layer, you can lessen the effect of the settings you create in the adjustment layer dialog box.

3 The new adjustment layer appears in the Layers panel, as the active layer. The

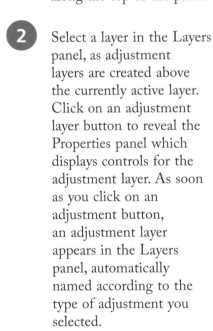

...cont'd

settings you create now apply to all layers below the adjustment layer.

4 As an alternative, you can click the Create New Fill or Adjustment Layer button ( ) at the bottom of the Layers panel, then choose an adjustment layer type. The adjustment layer appears above the previously active layer, and the appropriate controls appear in the Properties panel.

5 Click the Visibility button ( ) to the left of the adjustment layer, in the Layers panel, or at the bottom of the Adjustments panel, to hide/show the results of the adjustment layer settings.

6 Click another adjustment layer button in the Adjustments panel if you want to add further adjustment layers. To return to editing settings, for an existing adjustment layer, double-click the adjustment layer icon in the Layers panel – the appropriate adjustment controls appear in the Properties panel.

7 Some of the adjustment types have presets listed in the Properties panel. Click the Preset pop-up menu to reveal presets for an adjustment. When you click on a preset, the settings are applied as an adjustment layer, and the Properties panel displays the appropriate controls, according to the type of preset you selected.

Hot tip

To increase the size of the Properties panel, position your cursor on the bottom or left edge, or the corner of the panel. Click and drag when you see the cursor change to a bi-directional arrow:

Hot tip

If you create custom settings that you want to be able to reuse in the future, choose Save ... Preset from the Adjustments panel menu. It's a good idea to save the preset to the default folder within the Photoshop CS6 Presets folder. Give your preset a name, and make sure you leave the default file extension unchanged.

187

...cont'd

Don't forget

The adjustment layer settings do not have a permanent effect on pixels, until the layer is merged with other layers, or the image is flattened.

Hot tip

To limit the effect of the adjustment layer to the layer immediately below it, click the Clip to Layer button ( ) at the bottom of the Adjustments settings panel.

Hot tip

You can copy and paste adjustment layers between images, in order to apply consistent color and tonal changes to different images.

8 Click the on-canvas adjustment toggle button (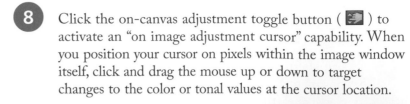) to activate an "on image adjustment cursor" capability. When you position your cursor on pixels within the image window itself, click and drag the mouse up or down to target changes to the color or tonal values at the cursor location.

9 Create a selection before you create an adjustment layer, to limit the effects of the adjustment layer settings to a specific area of an image.

10 After you make a change to settings in the Adjustment panel, the View Previous State button (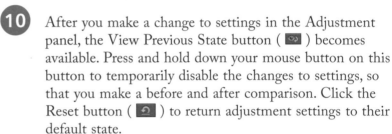) becomes available. Press and hold down your mouse button on this button to temporarily disable the changes to settings, so that you make a before and after comparison. Click the Reset button ( ) to return adjustment settings to their default state.

11 Drag the adjustment layer into the Trash can, if you want to discard the settings.

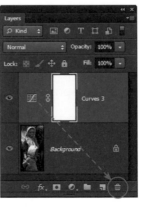

12 When you are ready to make the settings of the adjustment layer permanent, either use one of the Merge commands from the panel menu, or flatten the image.

Vibrance Adjustment

The Vibrance adjustment provides a method for enhancing color intensity in an image, without over saturating areas that are already saturated. This helps prevent creating colors that cannot be reproduced accurately.

1 Make sure the Adjustments panel is showing. Click once on the Vibrance adjustment icon. This displays settings for the adjustment in the Properties panel, and immediately creates a Vibrance adjustment layer in the Layers panel.

Hot tip

Using Vibrance can help avoid over-saturating skin tones in an image.

2 Drag the Vibrance slider to the right to increase color saturation, to the left to decrease it.

Hot tip

Create a selection before you create an adjustment layer if you want to create a layer mask, at the same time, that limits the effect of the adjustment to the selected area only; as in the screenshot opposite.

3 Drag the Saturation slider to increase or decrease saturation in all colors, regardless of their current level of saturation.

Color Balance

The Color Balance dialog box provides general controls for correcting an overall color cast in an image. As such, it provides the least complex method of color correction.

The Color Balance dialog box works on the principle of complementary colors. If there is too much cyan in an image, you drag the Cyan-Red slider towards red, to remove the cyan color cast. If there is too much magenta, drag the Magenta-Green slider towards green.

Don't forget

Set up a Color Balance adjustment layer by clicking the Color Balance button ( ), in the Adjustments panel, if you want to make non-destructive changes to the image. Using an adjustment layer, you can revise settings until you are ready to commit changes at a later stage.

1 To adjust the Color Balance of an image, choose Image > Adjustments > Color Balance. Click the Shadows, Midtones, or Highlights radio button to specify the tonal range that you want to make changes to.

2 Drag the color sliders to reduce/ increase the amount of a color in the image.

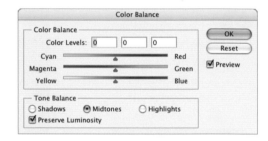

Don't forget

Work on the composite view of an image when using the Color Balance dialog box.

Beware

Use the Color Balance dialog box with caution, and only if your monitor is calibrated accurately, as you need to be certain that the color adjustments you see on screen accurately represent colors at final output.

Preserve Luminosity

Select this option to prevent brightness values from changing as you change color levels. This helps maintain the overall color balance in the image.

Black & White Command

For converting an image to black and white, the Black and White command offers much greater flexibility and control than using Image > Mode > Grayscale. By adjusting values for specific color components in the image, you can enhance or tone down areas of an image, as required.

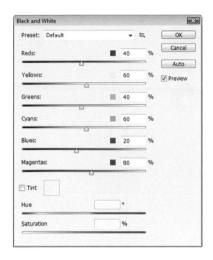

1 To convert an image to black and white, choose Image > Adjustments > Black and White.

2 Either select a preset conversion from the Preset pop-up menu, or use the color sliders to adjust the proportions of each color to be used in the conversion. Drag sliders to the right to darken and to the left to lighten the gray tones in the image.

3 If required, you can select the Tint checkbox to apply a color tone to the image. Drag the Hue slider to change the color of the tint. Use the Saturation slider to increase/decrease the amount or strength of the tint color.

You can use the Black and White command as an adjustment layer (see pages 186-187 for further information).

Click the Auto button to create a conversion that maximizes the distribution of gray values in the original image. You can then continue to adjust the sliders to achieve the final result you want.

191

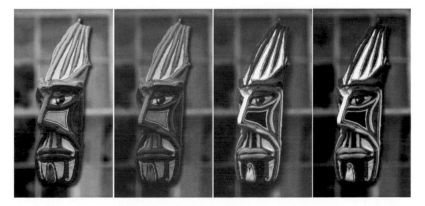

| Original | Image > Mode > Grayscale | Black & White (High Contrast Red preset) | Tint |

Position your cursor inside the image itself, then drag left or right to target and adjust specific color ranges within the image. If you are working with an adjustment layer, click the on-screen adjustment button (🔲) first.

Shadow/Highlight Command

The Shadow/Highlight command is useful for images with strong backlighting, resulting in a silhouette effect on the foreground elements. The default settings in the Shadow/Highlight dialog box are intended to improve images with backlighting problems. You can also use the Shadow/Highlight command to lighten shadows.

Hot tip

Make sure the Preview option is selected, to evaluate how changes you make to settings in the dialog box affect the image.

1 To adjust shadows and highlights in an image, choose Image > Adjustments > Shadow/Highlight.

2 Drag the Shadows Amount slider to the right, or enter a value in the percentage entry field, from 0-100, to lighten the shadows. The

higher the value, the greater the degree of lightening.

Hot tip

Choose Image > Adjustments > Photo Filter to access the Photo Filter dialog box. (The Photo Filters are also available in the Adjustments panel.) Photo filters simulate traditional photographic lens filters, used to warm or cool the overall color content of an image. The Warming (85) and Cooling (80) filters adjust the color temperature of an image. The Warming (81) and Cooling (82) filters are light balancing filters and have less impact on an image.

Use the Density slider to control the strength of the filter effect.

3 Drag the Highlights Amount slider to the right to darken the highlights. You can also enter a value in the percentage entry field. The higher the value, the greater the degree of darkening.

Before

After

13 Filters

Filters add enormous creative flexibility and potential to image manipulation, and it is well worth spending some time experimenting with them. You can use filters across an entire image, or you can apply them to selections or layers, to limit the results to specific areas.

Filter Controls

Hot tip

Click and hold on the preview window inside the filter's dialog box, to see the preview image without the filter settings applied.

Use the Filter menu to access the Photoshop filters. Many of the filters have standard controls, which are explained below. Some filters, such as Filter > Stylize > Solarize, do not display a dialog box, but apply the effect immediately. Other filters take you into the Filter Gallery dialog box, where you create and preview settings.

1 Click the Preview check box to see the effect of your settings previewed in the main image window, as well as in the Preview window inside the filter dialog box.

Hot tip

Choose Edit > Fade filter to reduce the effect of a filter on an image.

2 Click and drag on the image in the Preview window to scroll around to preview different parts of the image. Alternatively, with the filter's dialog box active, position your cursor in the main image window – the cursor

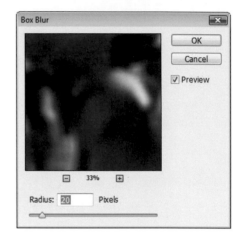

becomes a hollow box – then click to set the view in the Preview window.

3 Click the "+" or "-" buttons to zoom in or out on areas of the image. You can also use the Ctrl + Spacebar (Windows) or Command + Spacebar (Mac) keyboard shortcuts within the Preview window, or the image window.

4 Hold down Alt/option and click the Reset button (previously Cancel) to revert to the original settings in the dialog box.

Hot tip

Work with Smart Filters (see page 212) if you want to work non-destructively on an image. Smart Filters allow you to make changes to filter settings without changing actual pixel values in the image, until you are ready.

5 After you click OK on a filter's dialog box, use Ctrl + F (Windows) or Command + F (Mac) to reapply the last-used filter and its settings.

Unsharp Mask and Sharpen Filters

These filters allow you to enhance detail in your images.

Unsharp Mask

This is a powerful function that can help you to sharpen blurry images in specific areas. For example, if you rotate an image, or change the dimensions or resolution of the image, it may blur, due to any interpolation that Photoshop applies. Where the Unsharp Mask filter finds edges (areas where there is a high degree of contrast), it increases the contrast between adjacent pixels. The result is to create an apparent improvement in the focus of the image.

1 To use Unsharp Mask to sharpen an image, choose Filter > Sharpen > Unsharp Mask. The Unsharp Mask dialog box appears.

2 Adjust settings for Amount, Radius, and Threshold. Evaluate changes you make to settings in the Preview window, within the dialog box and in the image window itself. Click OK, or press Return/Enter.

Set the zoom percentage of the document window to 100%, to get an accurate preview of the effect of sharpening in the image. Also, it is preferable to evaluate final results in the actual document window, rather than in the Unsharp Mask preview window.

Amount – Use this to control the amount of sharpening applied to the edges (minimum = 1, maximum = 500). The picture will become pixelated if the amount is too high.

Values below 50% produce subtle results; values between 50% and 200% produce moderate results; while values between 200% and 500% produce dramatic, exaggerated results.

The settings for Radius and Threshold need to be taken into account when setting the Amount value (see page 196).

...cont'd

Radius – Radius controls the depth of pixels along the high-contrast edges that are changed.

A low radius value restricts the impact of the filter; higher values distribute the impact. Radius values of 2.0 or lower usually produce acceptable sharpening.

Threshold – Sets a level for the minimum amount of contrast between pixels an area must have before it will be modified. The Threshold value is the difference between two adjacent pixels – as measured in brightness levels – that must occur for Photoshop to recognize them as an edge.

High Threshold values limit changes to areas where there is a high degree of color difference. Use low values to apply the filter more generally throughout the image.

Sharpen and Sharpen More

Use the Sharpen and Sharpen More filters when an image becomes blurred after resampling. Both filters work by increasing contrast between adjacent pixels throughout the image, or selection. Sharpen More has a more pronounced effect than Sharpen.

Sharpen Edges

This filter has a more specific effect, applying sharpening along high-contrast edges. It has a less global impact on a selection or image than Sharpen and Sharpen More.

On high-resolution images, use a Threshold value of around 8 or higher to limit the sharpening effect to specific areas.

196

Sharpening works by increasing contrast where there is already edge detail. Using too much Sharpening in an image can cause halos, and other unwanted artifacts, to appear in the image.

Sharpen

Sharpen Edges

Sharpen More

Unsharp Mask

Smart Sharpen

The Smart Sharpen filter uses advanced algorithms to produce enhanced sharpening results, using an easy-to-use dialog box with an expanded Preview window, which makes it easier to evaluate the effect of settings on the image.

1 Choose Filter > Sharpen > Smart Sharpen.

2 Set values for Amount and Radius. Amount controls the degree of sharpening. Higher values increase the amount of contrast between neighboring pixels, producing the visual effect of increased sharpness between edge pixels in the image. Radius controls how far the results of sharpening extend into surrounding pixels.

3 Use the Reduce Noise slider to keep unwanted noise in the image to a minimum. High Reduce Noise values can reduce detail in the image. Typically, higher Amount settings will require higher Reduce Noise values.

4 Choose an option from the Remove pop-up menu. Each option uses a different algorithm to sharpen the image. Gaussian Blur uses the same method as the Unsharp Mask filter. Lens Blur attempts to detect detail, where it then increases sharpening, typically producing fewer halos. Use Motion Blur to lessen blur caused by movement of the subject. When you select Motion Blur, set the angle control to specify the direction of the blur.

Hot tip

Noise can appear in an image as areas of pixel variation, or color artifacts, which do not represent detail in the image, and are therefore undesirable.

Image noise typically appears either as luminance noise, which tends to make the image appear patchy, or color noise, where irregular color artifacts appear in the image.

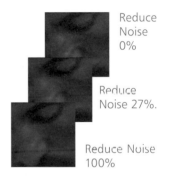

Reduce Noise 0%

Reduce Noise 27%.

Reduce Noise 100%

Hot tip

To achieve greater control over sharpening in shadow and highlight areas of an image, click the Expand Shadows / Highlights button. Use the Fade slider in the Highlights and/or Shadows tabs to reduce the overall impact of the sharpening settings, specifically in the shadow and highlight tonal ranges.

Blur Filters

Beware

The Blur More filter produces an effect roughly three times stronger than the Blur filter.

The Blur filters reduce the contrast between adjacent pixels along edges where considerable color shifts occur, to create a softening, defocusing effect. Blurring produces the opposite effect to sharpening – which increases the contrast between adjacent pixels.

"Blur" and "Blur More" blur a selection in preset amounts, offering only a limited degree of control. For greater control when blurring, you can use the Gaussian Blur option, which blurs according to a bell-shaped Gaussian distribution curve.

To Blur a Layer or Selection

1 Create a selection if you want to limit the effect of the Blur filter to a specific area of your image. Choose Filter > Blur > Blur, or Filter > Blur > Blur More.

Motion Blur
You can use Motion Blur to create the effect of a moving subject or camera.

Angle = 0,
Distance = 12

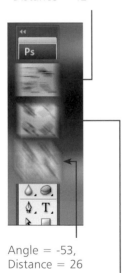

Angle = -53,
Distance = 26

Angle = -45,
Distance = 12

1 To create a motion blur, make a selection, if required. Choose Filter > Blur > Motion Blur.

2 Enter a value in the Angle box, or drag the Angle indicator to specify the angle or direction of the blur. Enter a value in the Distance entry box, to specify the distance in pixels for the blur effect. Click OK in the dialog box.

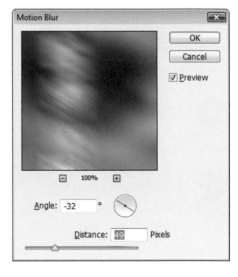

Motion Blur

OK

Cancel

☑ Preview

100%

Angle: -32 °

Distance: 49 Pixels

Radial Blur

Radial Blur creates the effect of zooming in as you take a picture.

1 To create a radial blur, make a selection, if required. Choose Filter > Blur > Radial Blur.

2 Select a Blur Method and Quality, and specify an Amount (0-100). Click and drag in the Blur Center window to specify the center point for the zoom or spin effect. Click OK in the dialog box.

If you are working on a layer, make sure the Transparency lock is deselected, if you want the blur to take effect along the edges of the layer's pixels (see page 123).

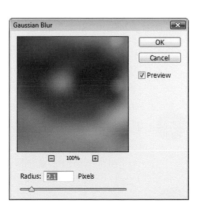

Amount – This value determines the distance pixels are moved to create the blur effect. Higher values produce more intense effects.

Zoom – Zoom creates a zoom-like blurring effect.

Spin – Spin rotates and blurs pixels around a central point.

Quality – Good and Best produce better, smoother results, due to the interpolation methods used, but take longer.

Gaussian Blur

1 Use Gaussian Blur to control the degree of blurring. Gaussian Blur adds low frequency detail to the image or selection. Choose Filter > Blur > Gaussian. Use the Radius slider to adjust the amount of blurring.

The Box Blur filter blurs an image or selection, using an average color value for neighboring pixels. Increased radius settings create greater blurring. This filter can produce interesting creative effects.

Path and Spin Blur

Create interesting motion blur effect using the Path and Spin blur filters in the Blur Gallery. You can use on-screen overlay controls or the blur settings in the Blur Tools panel on the right of the window to create the effects you want.

Hot tip

Click the Remove All Pins button in the Options bar to remove all blur effects. To return to creating settings for a blur effect, click the Expand/Collapse triangle twice: first to hide, then to show the settings for the blur type you are working with.

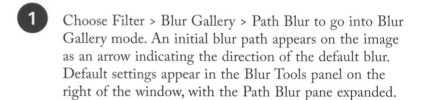

Path Blur

Use Path Blur to create a blur along user defined paths. You can have more than one path blur on the same image content.

1 Choose Filter > Blur Gallery > Path Blur to go into Blur Gallery mode. An initial blur path appears on the image as an arrow indicating the direction of the default blur. Default settings appear in the Blur Tools panel on the right of the window, with the Path Blur pane expanded.

Hot tip

To hide the path blur overlay controls, click the collapse triangle (▼) for Path Blur in the Blur Tools panel. The blur settings remain in force. Click the checkbox (✓)to the right of Path Blur to switch the settings off and on.

To delete a blur path, make sure it is selected, then press the Delete key.

2 To change the direction of the blur path, click and drag either the start or end pin. To create a curved blur path, click and drag the center pin on the blur path arrow.

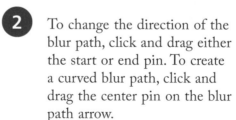

3 Experiment with controls in the Path Blur panel to create the effect you want. Hover your cursor over each control to get a tool tip explanation for the control.

4 When you are ready, click the OK button to accept the

blur settings, or click the Cancel button to return to the image without making changes.

Spin Blur

Use Spin blur to rotate and blur image content around a central reference point. You can define more than one spin blur in an image.

1 To create a spin blur, choose Filter > Blur Gallery > Spin Blur. An initial spin blur radius appears on the image. Default settings appear in the Spin Blur pane on the right of the window.

2 To reposition the blur radius, position your cursor in the middle of the radius, then click and drag the center pin that appears.

3 Use the Blur Angle slider in the Spin Blur pane to control the strength of the blur effect. Or, position your cursor at the center point of the blur, then click and drag in a circular direction on the on-screen outer gray Blur Angle control.

4 To change the size of the blur radius in proportion, position your cursor on the radius edge. Click and drag when the bi-directional arrow appears.

5 Drag the small white Elliptical handles on the edge of the blur radius to create an elliptical blur effect. Click and drag the larger, white Feather handles to control the distance over which the radial blur fades into the unblurred areas of the image.

Hot tip

Hold down H on the keyboard to temporarily hide the display of the on-screen overlay controls.

Hot tip

To delete a spin blur, make sure the blur radius is selected, then press the Delete key.

201

Hot tip

You can use controls in the Motion Blur Effects tab to create strobe like effects:

Noise Filters

Add Noise filter

The Add Noise filter randomly distributes high-contrast pixels in an image, creating a grainy effect.

You can use Add Noise to reduce banding in graduated fills.

Add Noise is a good way to begin creating textured backgrounds.

 To add noise, create a selection, select a layer or work on the entire image. Choose Filter > Noise > Add Noise. Specify Amount, Distribution, and Monochromatic options.

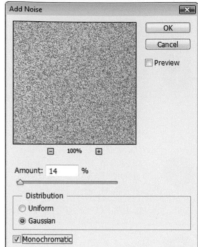

Amount – Determines the degree to which pixels are changed from their original color. Enter a number from 1-400.

Uniform – Produces an even spread of pixels.

Gaussian – Produces a more dramatic result.

Monochromatic – Choose Monochromatic to distribute grayscale dots.

Original gradient background

Amount = 20, Uniform, Monochromatic

Amount = 20, Gaussian, Monochromatic

...cont'd

Dust & Scratches filter

Use the Dust & Scratches filter to remove small imperfections and blemishes in a scan, caused by dust and scratches. The degree of success you have with this filter depends largely on the image or selection you apply it to.

1 To remove dust and scratches, create a selection or work on the entire image. Choose Filters > Noise > Dust & Scratches. Specify Radius and Threshold settings. Click OK.

Radius and Threshold settings are interdependent, and both are taken into account before changes are made.

Radius – Determines how small a blemish must be for it to be worked upon by the filter. For example, at a radius of 3 pixels, the Dust & Scratches filter will not attempt to make changes to imperfections above this size.

Threshold – Specifies the minimum amount of contrast between pixels there must be before changes are made.

Despeckle filter

This produces the opposite effect to the Add Noise filter, smoothing and blurring the image, but having little effect on edges.

Median filter

The Median filter also removes noise from a poor-quality scan. It works by averaging the color of adjacent pixels in an image.

1 To use the Median filter, create a selection, or work on the entire image. Choose Filter > Noise > Median. Specify a Radius value (1-100). Click OK in the dialog box.

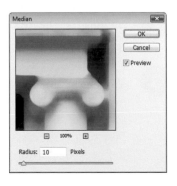

203

Automatic Camera Shake Reduction

For images that are correctly focused, but where there is slight blurring caused by camera shake or movement of the subject, the Camera Shake Reduction filter can improve the image by automatically detecting and then reducing the amount of blurring.

Hot tip

Choose Filter > Convert for Smart Filters before you use the Shake Reduction filter so that the changes you make are not permanently fixed, allowing you to re-edit settings at a later stage.

1 Choose Filter > Sharpen > Shake Reduction. Photoshop automatically detects an area of the image where shake reduction will have optimal effect – defining a blur trace region, indicated by the dotted rectangle. It also analyzes the type of blurring and makes automatic adjustments to reduce blurring.

Hot tip

Artifacts are clusters of pixels that create areas of undesirable, visually disruptive detail. Select the Artifact Suppression checkbox, and use the Artifact Suppression slider if necessary, to reduce the occurrence of artifacts.

Hot tip

If you are not satisfied with the automatic settings applied to the image, try increasing/decreasing the strength of the Blur Trace Settings, erring on the side of caution until you're familiar with the settings.

2 Switch the Preview checkbox off/on to see before/after Camera Shake Reduction versions of the image.

3 You can manually define the blur trace region. To reposition the region, drag the center pin (⊙). Drag the resize handles (-o-) to make it bigger or smaller. For best results define a region in the image which has well-defined edge contrast detail.

The Liquify Dialog Box

The Liquify dialog box allows you to create a wide variety of distortions, for retouching images or for achieving creative effects. The dialog box has tools that can push, pull, rotate, pucker, and bloat areas of the image. The Advanced Mode checkbox to the right of the Liquify window allows you to display further advanced Liquify tools and controls.

1 To distort an entire layer, select the layer, or make a selection on a layer to define an area for distortion. Choose Filter > Liquify.

2 Freeze areas of the image that you don't want to change, using the Freeze Mask tool. Set a Brush size, then drag across areas of the image you want to freeze. Frozen areas appear as a semi-transparent, red mask. Use the Thaw Mask tool to make frozen areas editable again.

3 Select a distortion tool, then set tool options (see page 206 for information on the tools). Choose a brush size from the Brush Size slider.

Set a brush pressure. Lower pressure settings distort the image more slowly, allowing you more control over the distortion. Brush Density controls the softness of the edge of the brush.

4 Drag in the image to create the distortion. You can press the left mouse button without dragging the mouse, to create effects with tools, such as the Twirl tools. Set a Brush Rate to control the speed at which distortions happen when you keep the mouse still. Click OK to accept the changes.

Use the Zoom and Hand tools as you would in the standard Photoshop image window.

The Smooth, Twirl Clockwise, Freeze Mask and Thaw Mask tools become available when you select the Advanced checkbox:

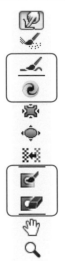

You must rasterize a Type layer, or a Shape layer, before you can use the Liquify command.

Liquify Distortion Tools

There are five distortion tools to choose from. Remember to create tool settings for Brush size and Brush Pressure before you use the tools. Advanced controls are available for Brush Rate and Brush Density. Distortions are most pronounced at the center of the brush area. You can create distortions by dragging across pixels, or simply by holding down the left mouse button.

Hot tip

Use the Reconstruct tool to restore pixels to their original state by dragging in the image preview:

This can be especially useful when you want to gradually reduce the amount of liquify without returning to the initial state of the image.

Hot tip

Click the Restore All button to revert to the original state of the image:

Reconstruct Options
Restore All

Hot tip

To undo/redo edits in the Liquify dialog box, use the keyboard shortcuts: Alt/option + Ctrl/Command + Z (Step Backward) or Shift + Ctrl/Command + Z (Step Forward).

1 Use the Forward Warp tool to distort pixels in a forward direction as you drag.

2 Use the Twirl Clockwise tool to rotate pixels around the brush area in a clockwise direction. Hold down Alt/option to twirl in a counter-clockwise direction.

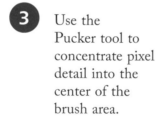

3 Use the Pucker tool to concentrate pixel detail into the center of the brush area.

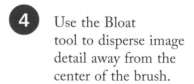

4 Use the Bloat tool to disperse image detail away from the center of the brush.

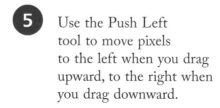

5 Use the Push Left tool to move pixels to the left when you drag upward, to the right when you drag downward.

Filter Gallery

The Filter Gallery allows you to preview and apply individual or multiple filter effects to an entire image, a layer, or a selection.

1 To show the Filter Gallery, choose Filter > Filter Gallery. A preview of the image, with the currently selected filter applied, appears on the left of the window.

The Filter Gallery is not available for images in CMYK color mode.

Not all Photoshop filters are available from within the Filter Gallery.

2 Click the Reveal/Hide triangle (▷) for each filter category, to show or hide the filters available for that category.

3 Click a filter thumbnail to apply it to the preview. Use the individual controls, on the right hand side of the window, to experiment and create the settings you want to use. Each filter effect has its own, specific set of controls.

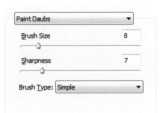

4 In the Preview area, use the "-" or "+" buttons, or the zoom pop-up, to zoom in or out on an area

of the preview. Position your cursor in the preview area, then click and drag to reposition the preview.

...cont'd

Hot tip

The Convert for Smart Filters command in the Filter menu allows you to apply filters to your image "non-destructively" – you can go back and make changes to the filter settings at a later stage. (See page 210.)

5 Use the Reveal/Hide button (⊗) to hide the filter thumbnails area to create a larger preview area, if necessary. You can choose filters by name from the Filter drop-down menu, if you hide the thumbnails.

6 To apply more than one filter to the preview, click the New Effect button (🔲) at the bottom of the window, then click on another filter effect thumbnail. The new filter is added to the bottom of the filter effect list.

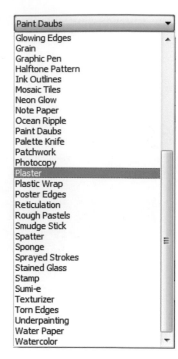

7 In the Filter effect list area, click a Visibility button to apply or hide the filter effect. Drag the filter effect upward or downward, to change the order in which the filters are applied. Drag a filter effect into the Trash can to remove it.

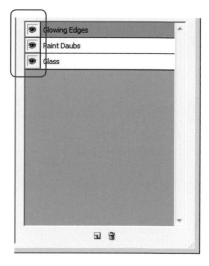

8 Click OK in the Filter Gallery dialog box when you are ready to apply the settings.

Vanishing Point

The Vanishing Point filter makes it possible to maintain accurate and correct perspective, when you edit an image that contains perspective planes. Use the filter to define a perspective grid, or plane, to establish a vanishing point. You can then make edits within the grid that conform to the correct perspective.

1 To edit in perspective, choose Filter > Vanishing Point. To define a perspective grid, select the Create Plane tool.

2 Position your cursor on the image, then click to set the first node for the plane. Move your cursor to a new position (do not hold down the mouse button and drag). Click to set the next node. Repeat the process to set a third and fourth corner node. The grid appears in blue, in the Vanishing Point window.

3 A blue bounding box indicates a valid grid. If the grid or bounding box turns yellow or red as you create or edit it, there is a problem with the alignment of the perspective plane. Typically, the plane doesn't line up correctly with perspective in the image. To correct this, select the Edit Plane tool (), position your cursor on a corner node of the perspective grid, then adjust the grid to line up with elements in the image.

Hot tip

To delete a perspective grid, select the Edit Plane tool, then press the Backspace or Delete button.

Hot tip

Working with the Create Plane tool, use the Grid Size pop-up to specify the frequency of the grid:

Choose Show Edges, from the panel menu (▾≡), to control the visibility of the perspective grid.

Hot tip

Using the Create Plane tool, hold down Ctrl/ Command, then drag a center top/bottom, or center left/right node to define an additional perpendicular plane.

...cont'd

4 To change the size of the perspective grid rectangle, make sure you drag either the center left/right, or center top/ bottom handle.

Removing objects in perspective

Hot tip

The Stamp tool uses techniques and controls very similar to those used for the Clone Stamp and Healing Brush tools (see Chapter 6, "The Editing Tools", for further details).

1 Create a perspective grid, then select the Stamp tool. The grid disappears, to facilitate editing, but the bounding box remains visible. Create settings for the diameter, hardness, and opacity of the brush in the Options bar (see Chapter 5, "The Painting Tools", for information on these controls).

2 Position your cursor over the source pixels – the area you want to use as a sample point. Hold down Alt/option, then click the mouse button to set the sample point, then release the Alt/option key.

3 Reposition your cursor over the target pixels – the area in the image where you want to paint out detail with pixels from around the sample point. Notice, as you move your cursor towards the rear of the perspective grid, that the cursor size changes to match the grid and maintain the correct perspective.

Hot tip

Use the Heal pop-up to specify a blending method for the sampled pixels. Select On to retain the texture of the sampled pixels and blend with the colors, lighting, and shading of the surrounding pixels in the target area. Select Luminance to retain the color of the sampled pixels and blend with the lighting of the pixels surrounding the target area.

4 Click and drag to remove unwanted detail. Repeat steps 2-4, if necessary, in order to use slightly different sample points, so that the result appears in keeping with the rest of the image, and as natural as possible.

Editing Perspective Planes

Using the Vanishing Point filter, you can create additional perspective planes that conform to the same perspective as the original plane. Initially, planes "tear off" at 90° angles. You can paste content into Vanishing Point, and manipulate it so that it conforms to the perspective grid.

1 Begin by creating the initial, or parent, perspective plane. Select the Edit Plane tool. Hold down Ctrl/Command, then drag a center left/right, or center top/bottom node to create a new, child plane at 90°.

2 If you need to change the angle of the new plane, to match the content of the image, enter an angle in the Angle entry box, or drag the Angle slider. To adjust the angle manually, hold down Alt/option, then drag the center node opposite the axis of rotation.

3 To paste content into perspective planes defined in Vanishing Point, make sure you copy the content to the clipboard before you choose Filter > Vanishing Point. When you paste content into Vanishing Point, it appears as a "floating" selection. Drag the selection into a plane, and it transforms into perspective. Click outside the selection to deselect it and apply the perspective transformation.

When you have overlapping planes in Vanishing Point, use Ctrl/Command + click to select through planes in the stacking order.

211

You cannot change the angle of a "parent" perspective plane after you create a "child" plane from it.

You must first rasterize a Type layer (Type > Rasterize Type) before you can paste it into a perspective plane.

Smart Filters

Smart Filters work with Smart Object layers. Using Smart Filters, you can work with filters non-destructively on an image – making changes to the filter settings as often as required.

You cannot apply Liquify and Vanishing Point filters as Smart Filters.

1 If you are working with an image consisting only of a background layer, duplicate the layer first. Otherwise, select the layer you want to apply a smart filter to.

2 Choose Filter > Convert for Smart Filters. This converts the layer into a smart object layer, to which you can then apply smart filters.

You can apply more than one filter as a smart filter.

3 Apply a filter from the Filter menu. The smart filter icon appears on the smart object layer, to indicate the presence of smart filters. The smart filter layer mask icon and the smart filter appear in the layers panel, below the smart object layer to which they are applied. Click the Expand/Collapse triangle to show/hide smart filters for the layer.

4 Double-click the smart filter name to edit the filter settings. Click the Visibility button (👁) to hide/show the smart filter settings on the image.

5 Using the smart filter layer mask, you can apply the smart filters selectively on the smart object layer. Make sure you click the layer mask icon to select it before you attempt to edit the layer mask. For example,
you could load a selection, then fill it with black to remove the smart filter effect in the area defined by the selection (see pages 172-173 for information on working with layer masks).

You can control opacity and blending mode for the smart filter by double-clicking the Edit Blending Options button (≡) for the smart filter layer.

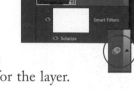

14 Web and Multimedia

This chapter looks at some of the considerations for using different image types effectively, in formats suited to the environment of the World Wide Web. It also covers techniques for using images in multimedia work.

You can use the keyboard shortcut, (Ctrl/Command + Alt/option + Shift + S), to go into the Save for Web dialog box.

Use the Zoom and Hand tools to change the magnification, and to scroll through images in the preview panes:

Save for Web

The Save for Web command offers comprehensive controls for saving images to be used on the Web. Use the Save for Web command when you want to create an image file size that is as small as possible – to ensure the fastest possible download times – without sacrificing too much quality.

1 Choose File > Save to save any changes you have made to the image in the current file format. Then choose File > Save for Web.

2 In the Save for Web dialog box, click the 2-Up tab to compare the original image, and the image with optimization settings applied. Click the Optimized tab to view the image with optimization settings applied. When viewing 2-Up and 4-Up, each optimized pane indicates file format, size, and approximate download time for a specific connection speed, in the annotations area.

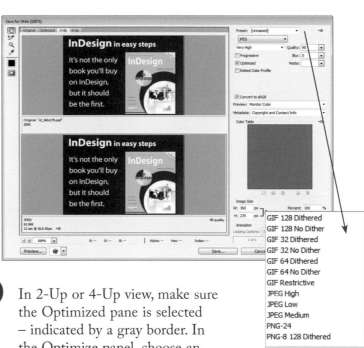

3 In 2-Up or 4-Up view, make sure the Optimized pane is selected – indicated by a gray border. In the Optimize panel, choose an optimization level from the Presets pop-up menu. The Optimized image pane updates, so that you can evaluate different options.

4 In 4-Up view, when you change the optimization settings for the Optimized pane, choose Repopulate Views, from the Presets panel menu, to update the remaining panes with lower-quality optimization settings.

Optimization: 4-Up View

The 4-Up tab is particularly useful, because it allows you to preview images using a variety of optimization levels, before you decide which level of optimization you want.

1 Click the 4-Up tab to view the Original image, the image optimized using the current optimization settings, set in the Optimization panel, and two lower-quality variations of the current optimization settings.

2 To use one of the lower-quality comparison panes as the Optimized image, click inside the pane to select it. A gray highlight border on the pane indicates that it is selected. Choose Repopulate Views, from the Optimization panel pop-up menu. The selected pane becomes the Optimized image. Its optimization settings appear in the Optimization area. The comparison panes update with lower-quality optimization settings.

3 To compare different, unrelated, optimization settings, click on a comparison pane to select it, then choose an optimization setting from the Settings pop-up. In this case, make sure you do not use the Repopulate Views command.

The arrangement of the 4-Up panes varies according to the size of the Save for Web dialog box, and the dimensions and orientation of the image.

For an image that contains slices, click the Slice Visibility button to view the slices in the Save for Web dialog box:

Saving Optimized Images

You can preview an optimized image in a web browser before you make a final decision on which optimization settings to use. This can be a useful check before committing yourself to saving the file.

Hot tip

To specify the browsers you want to use to preview optimized images, click the Browser pop-up menu then select Edit List:

In the Browsers dialog box, click the Add button, then navigate to the Program Files folder (Win), or the Applications folder (Mac) to locate the browser you want to use:

Select the Application file (.exe) for the browser, then click the Open button to add it to the Browsers dialog box. Repeat the process to add further browsers.

Click OK in the Browsers dialog box to add the browsers to the Browser pop-up list in the Save for Web dialog box:

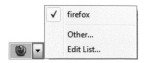

1 Choose a browser from the Browser Preview pop-up, from the bottom of the dialog box. The browser launches and displays the image from the selected pane. Image details, such as file format, dimensions, and file size are listed below the image. Below the image detail is the HTML code necessary to display the image.

2 To save an optimized image, select the pane with the settings you want to use. Click Save, in the Save for Web dialog box.

3 Use standard Windows/ Macintosh techniques to navigate to the folder in which you want to save the image. Enter a file name for the image. The file extension for the optimization settings is automatically appended to the file name. The file is saved using the current settings in the Optimize panel.

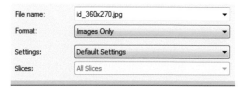

4 Select HTML and Images from the Format pop-up menu, to generate the code necessary to display the

...cont'd

image in a separate
HTML file. This
file is automatically
named and saved in
a folder you specify.
The optimized
image is saved in an
images folder, which
Photoshop creates
automatically within
the same folder.

5 To specify whether
the HTML file uses
a table, or Cascading
Style Sheets, to display
an image with slices,
choose Other from the
Settings pop-up menu.
Choose Slices from the
pop-up menu. Create
the settings you require
in the Slice Output
area of the Output
Settings dialog box.

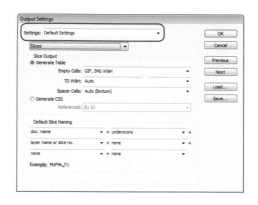

6 For images that contain slices, use the Slices pop-up
menu to choose whether to save all slices in the image, or
only the currently selected slice. Each slice is saved as a
separate file, and named according to the settings in the
Output Settings dialog box.

7 To change the way in
which slices are named,
in the Output Settings
dialog box choose
Saving Files from the
pop-up menu. Use the
File Naming pop-ups to
make changes.

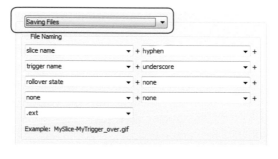

GIF Optimization Settings

The GIF file format usually provides the most efficient and flexible optimization controls, for images which have areas of flat color with sharp edges, and type, as you often find in logos and buttons.

1 To optimize an image, using GIF file format, select the image pane you want to create the settings for. To create a setting for a slice, use the Slice Select tool to select a slice.

2 Choose one of the preset GIF settings from the Preset pop-up menu. Or to create custom GIF settings, choose GIF from the Format pop-up, then specify settings using the options in the panel.

3 Drag the pop-up Lossy slider, or enter a value, to reduce file size by discarding color information. Values of 5-10 can often be applied without noticeably degrading the image quality. Choose a color palette (see pages 221), and a dither method (see page 222).

4 Use the Colors pop-up menu to specify the maximum number of colors in the Color palette. Increase the Web Snap setting, to shift colors to their closest Web palette equivalents, to help avoid dithering in a browser.

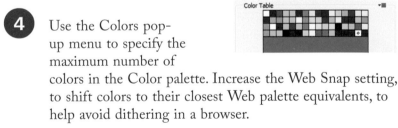

5 Select Transparency, to preserve any transparent areas in the image. You can choose a Matte color if you want to blend the edges of transparent areas into the background of a Web page. Use the Transparency pop-up to choose a dither type for the blended areas, if required.

You cannot use the Lossy option with the Interlaced option, or with a Noise or Pattern dither.

The Interlaced option creates an image that first downloads as a low-resolution preview, whilst the full file information is downloaded.

Avoid using GIF format if your image contains a gradient. Use JPEG format instead (see page 219).

JPEG Optimization Settings

JPEG optimization works best on continuous-tone images, such as photographs. JPEG compression can preserve more detail in photographic-type images than GIF, and still provide considerable file size reduction.

JPEG compression is "lossy". In order to make the file size of an image smaller, some image data is discarded, reducing the quality of the image.

1 To optimize an image using JPEG file format, select the image pane you want to create the settings for. To create a setting for a slice, use the Slice Select tool to select a slice.

2 Choose one of the preset JPEG settings from the Preset pop-up menu. Or create custom JPEG settings by choosing JPEG from the format pop-up, then specify settings using options in the panel.

3 Use the Quality pop-up to choose a quality setting, or drag the pop-up Quality slider. Use a high setting to preserve most

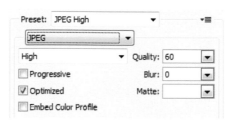

of the detail in the image, with a larger file size. Reduce the quality setting to achieve greater compression and a smaller file size, but with reduced image quality.

4 Select the Optimized checkbox, to create JPEGs with a slightly smaller file size. Some older browsers do not recognize this setting. Choose Progressive to cause the image to download to the browser in a number of passes, each pass building more detail into the image, until it downloads completely. Use Blur settings, if required, to allow greater compression on the file. Settings of less than 0.5 are recommended.

5 JPEG compression does not support transparency in images. You can fill transparent areas with a Matte color, to simulate transparency, provided you know the background color against which the image will be viewed.

For medium to high JPEG compression settings, you can use a small Blur value, e.g. 0.1-0.5, to blur pattern artifacts that may appear along sharp edges. Higher values may noticeably reduce image detail.

PNG File Format

PNG is a relatively new file format for saving images for use on the Web. There are two PNG file format options: PNG-8 and PNG-24.

PNG-8

PNG-8 file format uses 8-bit color, which allows a maximum of 256 colors in an image. It is most effective at compressing areas of solid, flat color, typically found in line art, logos, and illustrations with type.

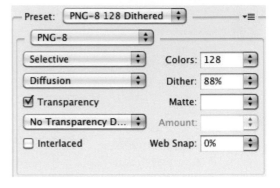

PNG-8 is a lossless compression formula – no color information is lost during compression. Depending on the image, PNG-8 compression can produce files 10-20% smaller than the same image compressed using GIF format.

PNG-8 file format can support background transparency, and background matting. Background matting enables you to blend the edges of an image into the background color you set as the background color of your web page.

PNG-24

PNG-24 supports 24-bit color, which allows millions of colors in the image. Like JPEG, this is a good format when you want to preserve subtle transitions in tone and color, in a photographic type image.

PNG-24 uses a lossless compression formula – no color information is discarded during compression. As a result, PNG-24 file sizes are typically larger than if you save the image using JPEG file format.

PNG-24 supports background transparency, and background matting. PNG-24 also supports multilevel transparency, which allows greater control over the way in which an image blends into the background color of a web page.

Hot tip

For images that use a very limited range of colors, the GIF format can produce smaller file sizes than PNG-8. Use the 4-Up tab when saving images, to choose the best optimization level.

Beware

Multilevel transparency is not supported by all browsers.

Color Palettes

A color palette controls the 256 possible colors that exist in an Indexed Color, GIF, or PNG-8 image. Photoshop uses three methods to create color tables in images: dynamic, fixed, and custom.

System palettes
This is the standard, 8-bit system palette of either the Macintosh or Windows system.

Exact
If the image you are converting already has fewer than 256 colors, Exact is the default. The actual number of colors is indicated in the Colors entry box. You cannot dither an Exact palette.

Restrictive (Web)
This is a palette reduced to 216 or fewer colors. Use this palette to achieve consistency across different platforms, and when you want to use more than one image on the same web page. Images based on different color palettes can look artificial when seen side-by-side.

Uniform
This palette is based on a uniform sampling of colors from the color spectrum.

Adaptive
This palette is built around the colors that actually occur in an image. For individual images, it gives better results than the web option, as the color table is created by sampling colors from the most frequently occurring areas of the color spectrum in the image.

Custom
This option allows you to create your own custom color table. You can add colors (⊡), lock colors (🔒), as well as map colors to their nearest web-safe color (🌐), or transparency (▣), using the buttons at the bottom of the Color Table palette.

Perceptual
The Perceptual option creates a color palette biased towards colors to which the human eye is most sensitive.

Selective
This is similar to Perceptual, but biased towards broad areas of color in the image, and also the preservation of web colors. Selective is the default.

Use the Color palette pop-up menu, in the settings area of the Save for Web dialog box, to select a color palette when optimizing images.

Dynamic – Perceptual, Selective, and Adaptive color palettes are created dynamically. Each time you optimize the image, the palette created is based on the colors occurring in the image. Different images generate different palettes.

Fixed – the Web, Mac OS, Windows, Black & White, and Grayscale color palettes are fixed. There is a limited, or fixed set of colors. If your optimization settings specify fewer than 256 colors, this reduced range of colors is drawn from the fixed color table.

Custom – Custom palettes use colors created or modified by the user. Existing GIF and PNG-8 files also have custom palettes.

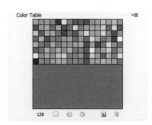

Dithering

Dithering is a technique used to simulate colors that are not actually in the color palette. On computer monitors that support only 256 colors, dithering takes place to simulate a greater range of colors in an image than the monitor is actually capable of displaying. For web images, this is referred to as browser dither.

Dithering juxtaposes pixels of different colors, to create the illusion of additional colors.

You can choose a dithering method for an image when you optimize it. This is referred to as application dither – the dither is built into the image.

Hot tip

You can minimize the occurrence of browser dither by creating the image using only web-safe colors.

1 For GIF images, in the Save for Web dialog box, choose an option from the Dither pop-up. For Diffusion, set a Dither Amount. Higher values result in more dithering, which creates the appearance of a greater number of colors in the image. Higher values can also increase the file size, depending on the image.

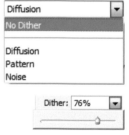

No Dither
No dithering is applied to the image.

Pattern
This creates a square dither pattern, similar to halftones, to simulate colors not available in the color table.

Diffusion
The results of Diffusion are usually less noticeable than Pattern, as the dithering is spread across a range of pixels.

Noise
Applies a random dither pattern. This option can be used for images with slices.

Images with areas of solid color may compress best with Dither set to None. Images with gradients usually need dithering to prevent obvious banding.

15 Animations and Slices

GIF animation and image slicing are two very powerful and flexible techniques, which can be used for World Wide Web and multimedia images.

Creating a Simple Animation

Animations can range from the very simple to the very complex. Try to keep your animations simple, at the outset. Remember that animation effects, if used indiscriminately on web pages, can be distracting and, as a result, lose their intended impact.

Hot tip

To avoid confusion as you create an animation, make sure that you have created and finished editing all the objects and layers you want to use, before you start to build the animation.

1 Create an image in Photoshop. Use layers as the basis for the animation. The layers you create form the basic building blocks for the animation. Put elements you want to animate on separate layers.

Hot tip

The first time you show the Timeline panel, click the Create Frame Animation button:

2 Hide any layers containing elements you do not want to appear at the start of the animation.

Hot tip

Choose Convert to Video Timeline from the Timeline panel menu to access the video style timeline. You can also click the Convert to Video Timeline button at the bottom of the Timeline panel:

You can click the Convert to Frame Animation button to change back to the default Timeline:

3 Choose Window > Timeline to show the Timeline panel. Photoshop adds an extra row of animation options to the Layers panel when you show the Timeline panel. The current state of the image appears as frame 1 in the panel.

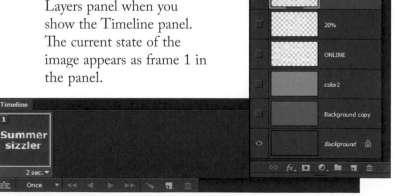

4 Choose New Frame from the panel's pop-up menu, or click the New Frame button. This creates frame 2, which is a duplicate of the preceding frame.

Animations are saved in the GIF file format. The JPEG and PNG formats cannot be used for animations.

5 Make a change to a layer. Changes you make to the layers, such as layer visibility, position, opacity, or layer effects, form the animation when the frames are viewed in quick succession. In this example, one text layer is hidden, and a different one is revealed.

6 Repeat Steps 4-5 as necessary.

Any changes you make on a layer, that affect actual pixel values – for example, painting, changing color or tone, or using transform commands – will affect all frames in the animation where the layer is present.

7 Save the animation in Photoshop format, as you build and make changes. This means you can return to the original file, if necessary, to make further adjustments (see page 228 for information on saving an optimized version of the animation for use on the World Wide Web).

225

Playing and Managing Frames

As you build an animation, you will need to preview it and to control aspects such as looping and frame rate.

Hot tip

To select multiple, consecutive frames, click on the first frame, hold down Shift, then click on the last frame in the range you want to select. To select non-consecutive frames, click on a frame to select it, hold down Ctrl/Command, then click on other frames to add them to the previously-selected frame.

1 To play an animation, click the Play button. The animation plays in the image window, and each frame in the Timeline panel highlights in sequence as the animation plays. Click the Stop button to stop the animation at the current frame.

2 To select a frame, click on the frame in the Timeline panel. The frame highlights and becomes the current frame. The current frame is displayed in the image window. It is the frame that can currently be edited.

3 To delete a frame, first click on it to select it. Then click the Trash can icon button at the bottom of the panel. Alternatively, drag the frame into the Trash can, or choose Delete Frame from the panel menu.

New Frame
Delete Frame
Delete Animation

Hot tip

When you select multiple frames, you can distinguish the current frame by the white highlight border around the frame:

4 To change the position of a frame, select the frame you want to move, then drag it to a new location. Release the mouse when you see a thick black bar at the position you want to move the frame to.

...cont'd

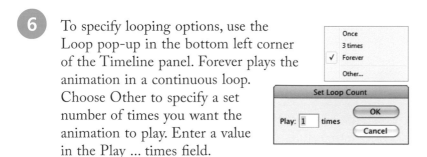

5 To set the frame delay rate (the speed at which frames advance), first select a frame, or multiple frames. Use the Frame Delay pop-up located below each frame. Either choose a value from the preset list, or choose Other, then specify a delay in the Set Frame Delay dialog box.

6 To specify looping options, use the Loop pop-up in the bottom left corner of the Timeline panel. Forever plays the animation in a continuous loop. Choose Other to specify a set number of times you want the animation to play. Enter a value in the Play ... times field.

Copying and pasting frames

You can copy a frame, or multiple frames, and then paste the copied frame(s) into a new location in the current animation, or into a completely different animation.

1 To copy a frame, first select the frame. A blue highlight indicates the frame is selected. Choose Copy Frame, from the Timeline panel menu (▤).

2 Select a frame at the location you want to paste the copied frame to. Choose Paste Frame, from the Timeline panel menu. Choose an option for Paste Method, then click OK.

Hot tip

For a selected range of frames, you can choose Reverse Frames from the panel menu to reverse the order of the frames. This would be useful after pasting the frames in the example below.

227

Optimize and Save Animations

To maintain consistent color across all frames in an animation, use either the Adaptive, Selective, or Perceptual color palette when creating your GIF optimization settings.

When you have created the frames for your animation, and you are satisfied with the effect, you can optimize and then save the animation.

1 To optimize an animation, choose Optimize Animation, from the Timeline panel menu. It is recommended that you leave both Optimize By options selected, to achieve the best quality optimization. Click OK.

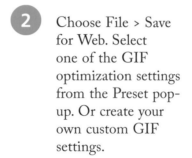

2 Choose File > Save for Web. Select one of the GIF optimization settings from the Preset pop-up. Or create your own custom GIF settings.

3 To preview the results of the optimization settings for different frames in the animation, from within the Save for Web dialog box, click the Previous/Next Frame, First/Last Frame buttons, or click the Play button to play all frames.

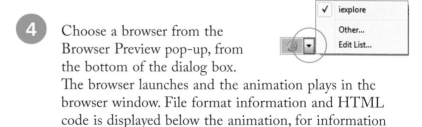

4 Choose a browser from the Browser Preview pop-up, from the bottom of the dialog box. The browser launches and the animation plays in the browser window. File format information and HTML code is displayed below the animation, for information purposes. Close the browser.

5 To save the animation, choose File > Save Optimized As. Specify a location and name for the file. The .GIF file extension is appended automatically.

Tweening

The Tween command allows you to create smooth animations, by creating additional frames between existing frames in the animation. These in-between frames create smoother movement.

1. To tween a frame, first click the New Frame button to create a duplicate of the first frame. Make a change (reposition an object, for example) to the layer on which you are working.

The term "tweening" is derived from a traditional animation term "in betweening", where additional frames were created between key frames to create smooth animation effects.

 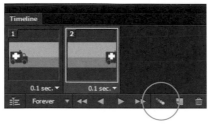

2. Click the Tween button ( ) in the Animations panel, or choose Tween from the panel pop-up menu.

3. For Layers, select the Selected Layer option, to vary only the currently selected layer in the selected frame, otherwise leave the option set to All Layers. Choose Parameters options to specify which elements you want to tween. In this example, it is important to choose Position, as it is the position of the layers in the animation that varies. Select Opacity and Layer Effects, if these vary between frames.

Use tweening to dramatically reduce the amount of time needed to create smooth animations.

4. Use the Tween With pop-up to choose the frame you want to tween the currently selected frame with. Enter a value in the Frames to Add field to specify the number of in-between frames. The more frames you add, the smoother the animation, but you get a larger file size.

Tweened animation frames do not require a new layer for each new frame. The tweening effect takes place on an individual layer.

5. Click OK in the dialog box. The in-between frames are added as new frames. Subsequent frames are renumbered accordingly.

Hot tip

The Slice and Slice Select tools are located in the Crop tool group.

Hot tip

As soon as you select the Slice tool, existing slices display automatically.

Hot tip

To use interactive alignment guides to align slices accurately, choose View > Show > Smart Guides. "Smart" alignment guides appear as you draw and move slices in an image with multiple layers, and/ or existing slices. To work effectively with smart guides, use them in conjunction with the Snap/Snap To options in the View menu.

Beware

When you use the Create Slices from Guides command, Photoshop deletes previously created slices.

Slicing Images

Slices are rectangular areas of an image that can be saved as separate, independent images, which can be used on the Web or in multimedia applications. An image initially consists of a single slice, by default, comprising the complete image. This becomes apparent when you select the Slice Select tool – a gray auto-slice icon (01 ⊠) appears in the top left corner of the image. When you create a new slice, the remainder of the image is automatically divided into further slices.

1   To create a slice using the Slice tool, click on the tool to select it. Position your cursor on the image, then drag to define the area of the slice. The slice you define is a User-slice (03 ⊠).

2   When you release the mouse, Photoshop automatically generates additional slices for the remaining areas of the image, which are not defined as User-slices. The additional slices are Auto-slices (01 ⊠).

Slices from guides

A quick, convenient technique for slicing an image is to create slices based on ruler guides you position in the image.

1   Drag in ruler guides to indicate where you want to create slices (see page 21 for information on creating ruler guides).

2   Select the Slice tool, then click the Slices From Guides button in the Options bar. The slices appear in the image. Each slice is numbered. Slices created from guides are User-slices (see page 231-232 for information on User- and Auto-slices).

Working with Slices

Use the following techniques to hide and show slices, and to manipulate them in a variety of ways.

Slices show automatically when you select the Slice Select tool.

1 To hide slices and slice information, such as slice number and slice type icons, choose View > Show > Slices. To show slices, choose the same option again, or select the Slice Select tool.

2 To select a User-slice, select the Slice Select tool. Click on a slice. A colored bounding box with eight selection handles appears around the slice, indicating it is selected.

3 To move a User-slice, select the Slice Select tool, position your cursor within the slice you want to move, and then drag the slice.

To delete a User-slice, first select it, and then press the Backspace or Delete key. Auto-slices are automatically created to fill the same area.

4 To resize a User-slice, select the Slice Select tool. Select a slice and then drag a side or corner resize handle.

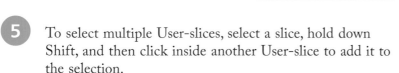

5 To select multiple User-slices, select a slice, hold down Shift, and then click inside another User-slice to add it to the selection.

User- and Auto-slices

A slice can have one of two statuses: User or Auto. There are more possibilities for modifying User-slices. Slices you create using guides, or the Slice tool, are User-slices. Slices created automatically by Photoshop are Auto-slices. An image automatically consists of one Auto-slice comprising the full image.

You can change or "promote" an Auto-slice into a User-slice. This is useful, as User-slices can be assigned different optimization settings. Auto-slices in an image are initially linked, and therefore share the same optimization settings. The link symbol ( ) on Auto-slices indicates that they share the same optimization settings.

To delete all slices in an image, choose View > Clear Slices.

...cont'd

Hot tip

User-slices have blue slice annotation symbols; Auto-slices have gray slice annotation symbols.

Hot tip

You can promote a selected Auto-slice to a User-slice by clicking the Promote button in the Options bar:

Don't forget

Photoshop can generate slices as an HTML table, or using Cascading Style Sheets. In the Save Optimized As dialog box (see page 234), click the Output settings button to specify which method is used.

There are two types of slices: Image or No Image. Image slices contain image information – pixels. No Image slices can contain a solid color, or HTML text. An Image slice is identified by the Image icon (⊠), when slices are visible.

Starting in the top left corner, slices are numbered from left to right and top to bottom. As you add, delete, and rearrange slices, slice numbers update automatically.

When selecting slices with the Slice Selection tool, User-slices are indicated by a solid boundary line and selection handles; Auto-slices by a dotted line.

Slice Options

The Slice Options dialog box enables you to set options, such as URLs, if you want to make slices into clickable buttons, as well as specifying whether slices are treated as an image, or as an area to be filled with a background color or HTML text.

1 To show the Slice Options dialog box, select a slice, then click the Slice Options button in the Options bar, or double-click inside the slice. The default slice name and slice number appear in the Name entry box. You can edit the slice name, if required.

2 To make a slice a clickable button, enter a URL in the URL entry field. You should include the http:// specifier at the beginning of the URL, for absolute paths. You can also specify relative paths. Enter the text you want to appear in the browser's status area, and supply text for the alt attribute of the image, if required.

Optimizing and Saving Slices

When you finish creating and adjusting slices, you can use the Save for Web dialog box to optimize and save individual slices, or complete images, for use on the Web.

1 To optimize slices in an image, choose File > Save for Web. Slice borders are visible by default. Click the Slices Visibility button in the toolbox on the left to hide/show slice borders, as required.

Unselected slices in the Save for Web dialog box appear slightly dimmed, to differentiate them visually from selected slices, which appear as normal. This dimmed color overlay has no effect on the actual appearance or color values of the image.

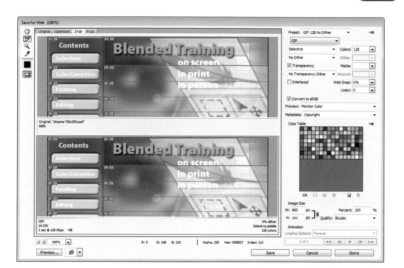

2 To select an individual slice to optimize, select the Slice Select tool, then click into a visible slice in the optimized pane. The selected slice appears at full strength, with a colored highlight border. To select multiple slices in order to apply consistent optimization settings, hold down Shift, and then click into additional slices to add them to the initial selection, or drag through the slices you want to select with the Slice Selection tool.

3 To easily reselect related groups of slices, first select two or more slices, then choose Link Slices, from the Optimize panel menu. The slice status icons (03 ⊠ §) appear in a different color, to indicate the link.

...cont'd

You can unlink individual, or all selected slices, using options in the panel menu.

Hot tip

Using the Slice Select tool, double-click on a slice to show the Slice Options dialog box.

4 Auto-slices are linked by default. When you apply optimization settings to an Auto-slice, the settings apply to all Auto-slices. If required, you can select an Auto-slice, then choose Unlink Slice, from the panel menu. This promotes the slice to a User-slice, which you can then optimize with individual settings.

5 Create the optimization settings you require for each slice in the image, using the Presets and/or the custom settings in the Optimization panel (see pages 216-217 for further information on optimizing images).

6 Click the Done button to return to the image, retaining any modified settings for the dialog box. Click the Save button to save the optimized slices.

Hot tip

To avoid the possibility of seams appearing between slices, when optimizing using GIF or PNG-8 formats, make sure you use the same color palette and dither settings, especially for adjacent slices.

7 In the Save Optimized As dialog box, select an option from the Slices pop-up menu. Choose Selected Slices, if you selected specific slices prior to clicking the Save button and you do not want to save all slices in the image (see pages 214-215 for further information on saving images).

239